JESUS PRESENT AND COMING

Jesus
PRESENT
and COMING

Daily meditations on the Advent and Christmas Masses

EMERIC LAWRENCE O.S.B.

The Liturgical Press
Collegeville, Minnesota

Nihil obstat: Robert C. Harren, J.C.L., *Censor deputatus.*
Imprimatur: ✛ George H. Speltz, D.D., Bishop of St. Cloud. September 13, 1982.

Cover by Sr. Mary Charles McGough, O.S.B.

Library of Congress Cataloging in Publication Data

Lawrence, Emeric Anthony, 1908–
  Jesus present and coming.

  1. Advent—Meditations.   2. Christmas—Meditations.
3. Bible—Liturgical lessons, English.   I. Title.
BV40.L38   1982   242'.33   82-20380
ISBN 0-8146-1284-9

CONTENTS

ADVENT

The title of this book is intended to give some idea of the meaning of Advent—or perhaps meanings, for praying through this holy season will help us to see that there is more than one. We do indeed look forward to and prepare for the celebration of the birth of Jesus at Christmas, and we spend four weeks listening to Isaiah's prophecies describing who and what the Savior will be, what he will do, and even the place of his birth and the approximate time. And more than once we are reminded that Christ will come again on the last day.

But we also know that the Jesus foretold by Isaiah has come, and the Gospels give the details of the birth, the kind of life he lived, climaxed by his death and resurrection. The Gospels also reveal that he established a Church on the apostles and appointed them to go and preach his Gospel to all peoples, to celebrate the sacraments, especially baptism and the Eucharist, and promised *to be with them* all days to the end of the world. We believe that he is still with the Church, that he is still what his name means, Emmanuel—"God is with us."

What then does Advent mean? What does it do? First, it does not ask us to *pretend* that we are living in pre-Christian times, looking forward with the Chosen People to the birth of the Messiah. Advent is definitely *not* an exercise of the imagination, of mere remembering. To be sure, we do read and meditate on the same Old Testament prophetic texts that gave and kept alive the hope and longing of the Jews. But now those texts belong to us. We clothe them with our hopes, our desires, longings, pains, and needs.

It is time to state clearly what liturgical celebration can and does do: it makes-present-again for us, here and now, the entire historical redeeming life, death, and resurrection of Jesus. Fr. Adrian Nocent, O.S.B., tells us that Vatican II affirmed the value of liturgical celebration as being the summit of the Church's activity: "The Church did so because it saw in that celebration the saving mysteries of Christ made present here and now, and rendered visible through signs. 'Summit of the Church's activity, and source of sanctification!' What a brilliant light radiated from those words!'' (*The Liturgical Year:* vol. 1 [Advent] Collegeville, Minn.: The Liturgical Press, 4).

Those of us who watch TV, especially sporting events, are familiar with the reality of ''instant replay.'' A play unfolds on the field or court, the camera records it, and in a flash is able to show it again, just as it happened. It may not be too exact—and it may even seem a little flippant—to compare our liturgical celebrations to this kind of instant replay. But that's what it really is . . . and more. It is reality. It is for *now.*

So we have a right, indeed, even a duty to look forward to and prepare for our celebration of the birth of Jesus at Christmas. The more and the better we prepare, the more Christmas will mean to us. The best way to prepare is to reflect on the texts of these Advent Masses and to heed the summons of John the Baptizer: ''Reform your lives! The reign of God is at hand. . . . Prepare the way of the Lord, make straight his paths. . . . Repent! Be converted!''

Advent is always a new beginning—for the Church and for each of us. It is a time for renewal, of growing in intimacy with Jesus and in an ever deeper understanding of him and his life in and for us. In a word, we look forward to and prepare for the Word being made flesh in our hearts and our lives so that he will truly be for us Emmanuel—''God is with us.''

At Christmas, Christ will reveal himself to us as the divine Bridegroom who, year after year, Advent after Advent, woos us with this proposal: ''Come, my people, be my beloved. My love can save you, rescue you from the hopelessness of life, help you to understand the cross you bear, bring comfort to your loneliness if you would only let it.'' Please God that some day, some Advent, that divine proposal will bring forth from us an irrevocable YES, and we will cry out to him: ''All my heart goes out to you, my God. To you I lift up my soul, I trust in you.''

The Cycles of Readings

There are three cycles of readings (from the Old Testament, from one of the New Testament Letters, and from the Gospels) for the Sundays of the Church year. The cycles begin with the first Sunday of Advent each year. Thus Cycle C begins in 1982 on November 28 and will continue on through the Sundays of 1983. Cycle C will return again in Advent 1985, 1988, 1991, etc. Cycle A begins with Advent 1983 and returns again in 1986 and 1989. Cycle B begins in Advent 1984 and returns in 1987, 1990, etc.

ACKNOWLEDGEMENTS

I am grateful to the sisters of St. Scholastica Priory for having favorably listened to much of the material in this book and for the encouragement they so generously provide my literary efforts. I am particularly grateful to Sr. Timothy Kirby, O.S.B., and to my colleague Fr. Angelo Zankl, O.S.B., for their valuable suggestions for improving these meditations. Thanks also to Sr. Mary Charles McGough, O.S.B., for again designing a cover and to the editors of The Liturgical Press for preparing the manuscript for publication.

Fr. Emeric A. Lawrence, O.S.B.
St. Scholastica Priory
Duluth, Minnesota

READING I   Isa 2:1-5   **READING II**   Rom 13:11-14
GOSPEL   Matt 24:37-44

Reading I: We enjoy Isaiah's vision of the messianic times when there will be universal peace.

Reading II: St. Paul tells us that the best way for us to prepare for Christ's coming to us at death and/or the end of time is to "put on the Lord Jesus Christ."

Gospel: Speaking of the end of the world, Jesus warns us to be prepared.

All the great themes of Advent come together in this First Sunday's liturgy: longing for God, conversion, preparation for Christmas, being ready to greet Christ when he comes again. There is even a program for implementing these themes, as we shall see. But the one idea that dominates this Sunday's readings is the Second Coming of Christ. "You cannot know the day your Lord is coming," Jesus tells us in the Gospel. "The Son of Man is coming at the time you least expect." The inevitable conclusion he wants us to draw is, of course, that we must be prepared. Prepared *now.* We cannot put it off.

It is obvious that the idea of the Second Coming is much more a reality to the Church than it is for the majority of us Christians. "Let us proclaim the mystery of faith," the priest tells us immediately after the consecration of the bread and the wine, and we may respond:

> Christ has died,
> Christ is risen,
> Christ will come again.

Or:

> Dying you restored our death,
> rising you restored our life.
> Lord Jesus, come in glory.

After the Lord's Prayer, we say or sing:

> . . . protect us from all anxiety
> as we wait in joyful hope
> for the coming of our Savior, Jesus Christ.

NOTE: Since only the Scripture references and short summaries of the readings are given here, I suggest that the reader look up the Scripture passages and read them thoughtfully before going on to the meditation.

We can wonder about the Church's vision here. Could it be that she realizes that the work of Christ, the redemption, will not be complete until evil is finally overcome, peace reigns universally and all humanity is reconciled with God? If that idea is hard to grasp, we can settle for the very practical conclusion that Christ will come to us at the moment of our death, and it behooves us to be prepared. "The Son of Man is coming at the time you least expect."

The question is: how does the Church want us to prepare ourselves? There was a time when priests used to preach "hellfire and damnation" sermons whenever the Gospel of the end of the world came. The idea was to try to frighten people into "being good." Some hurried to confession, and there was a momentary change in their lives. But usually it didn't last. The question is: Does God want to be served by fear-dominated slaves or by loving, respecting, yearning daughters and sons?

Today's Alternative Opening Prayer provides us with the best possible way of preparing to meet Christ when he comes again:

> Father . . . our hearts desire the warmth of your love
> and our minds are searching for the light of your Word.
> Increase our longing for Christ our Savior
> and give us the strength to grow in love,
> that the dawn of his coming
> may find us rejoicing in his presence
> and welcoming the light of his truth.

"Our hearts desire the warmth of your love . . . ." Do we need to prove that love is the deepest need of any human heart? Is any person ever satisfied with the depth and intensity of his or her love? Even on a human level—between spouses or sweethearts—people always want to love more and more; they always desire a deeper and deeper union with the beloved. This is even more the case when the beloved is God. And so we pray:

> Increase our longing for Christ our Savior
> and give us the strength to grow in love.

Longing is loving. Loving is longing.

Note that expression "the strength to grow in love." Loving is hard work. It requires all the power of the human heart . . . and more besides: strength from God.

Then comes the purpose, the goal, of all this praying:

> that the dawn of his coming
> may find us rejoicing in his presence . . . .

We are frozen by fear at the prospect of an unexpected surprise appearance, but we rejoice that he, the Lord Jesus, has already made himself at home in our minds and hearts and lives.

But we can't let this Mass go without some reflecting on Paul's advice to us today. Paul (mistakenly) believed that Jesus would come again in his own lifetime, and he shared this conviction with his followers. Accordingly, his message is both practical and deeply spiritual: "The night is far spent; the day draws near. Let us cast off the deeds of darkness and put on the armor of light. . . . put on the Lord Jesus Christ . . . ." (Reading II).

Paul talks as though Jesus is kind of a coat that we are supposed to "put on." What does he mean? Is Paul perhaps proposing something impossible for us poor humans? Can I by sheer human effort put on Jesus? Become like unto him? Become another Christ? Paul would be the last one in the world to think that way.

But what I can do, if I choose to, is to try to prepare this person who I am to be clothed with Christ by stripping myself of my unkind and unjust ways of thinking, judging, speaking, my self-indulgence and selfishness and say: "Here am I, you take over. Clothe me with yourself." I believe this is the way our Lady did it. She gives us her very own secret of holiness in her words: "Behold the handmaid of the Lord. Be it done to me according to thy word."

Perhaps one of these Advents we ought to give Mary's way a try. We'll never regret it. "To you, my God, I lift my soul, I trust in you; let me never come to shame" (Entrance Antiphon).

* * *

"Lord, let us see your kindness,
and grant us your salvation" (Gospel Verse).

"The Lord will shower his gifts,
and our land will yield its fruit" (Communion Antiphon).

NOTE: As a means for recalling the content of each daily meditation, I suggest that the reader *memorize* one of these texts and repeat it often during the day. This will help turn the entire day into a continuous prayer.

READING I   Isa 63:16-17, 19; 64:2-7   READING II   1 Cor 1:3-9
GOSPEL   Mark 13:33-37

Reading I: Isaiah prays to God in the name of all his people, asking for-
               giveness for their sins and placing their lives in his hands.

Reading II: St. Paul thanks God for his favors to the people and begs that
               the Lord will continue to strengthen them as they prepare for
               ''the day of the Lord.''

Gospel: We hear Mark's account of Christ's warning to the disciples
               to be ready for his Second Coming, for they know not the day
               nor the hour.

> Lord, make us turn to you,
> let us see your face and we shall be saved (Responsorial Psalm).

Reading Hebrew history, one has to conclude that the Jews really
knew how to sin. They were very good at it, at times dramatic and
spectacular, and always on a universal, national scale. But their
real greatness is that they also knew how to repent. And *as a nation*
they knew whom they had offended. They were nationally aware
that God in making them his Chosen People had made their sin all
the more enormous.

Another element in their greatness is that they had men of God,
called prophets, who knew how to call them to repentance and
were able to put their national sorrow and contrition into such magnificent and vivid word imagery. Isaiah was perhaps the greatest
and most talented of them all.

Every one of his lines in Reading I deserves our admiration and
reflection:

> You, Lord, are our father,
> our redeemer you are named forever.
> Why do you let us wander, O Lord, from your ways
> and harden our hearts so that we fear you not?

Words written long ago, but as true now as they were then. Human
persons use their God-given freedom to turn away from God and
then blame him for not having stopped them for having forsaken
him and his love! Do we want to be free or not? We want to be free;
we want God to heal us when we wound ourselves by sin, but we
seem to want him to do all the work. He'll do it, but only on condition that he gets some cooperation from us, some determination to
stay healthy.

There's a bit of mystery in all this, but let us not linger on it; rather let us go on to Isaiah's "general confession" in the name of his people:

> Behold, you are angry, and we are sinful;
> all of us have become like unclean men . . . .
> We have all withered like leaves,
> and our guilt carries us away like the wind.
> There is none who calls upon your name,
> who rouses himself to cling to you;
> For you have hidden your face from us
> and have delivered us up to our guilt.

It's not hard for us as individuals—maybe as parishes and families—to make that confession our very own. (It might be harder for us as a nation, since as a nation we hardly know God, hardly are aware of our obligations to him as our Creator and Lord. Moreover, we do not have prophets who can speak like Isaiah.) The word "guilt" occurs twice in that confession. Guilt is more than a sense of self-defeat rising out of a knowledge of having let our better selves down. True guilt comes from a realization of having deliberately, maybe even maliciously, used our freedom to choose our own will and way of life over against God and his will. It is a recognition of our having refused to accept his love and guidance for our lives. We want to live the way we want to, but find that that way leads only to defeat.

And so we come to the solution suggested by Isaiah:

> Yet, O Lord, you are our father;
> we are the clay and you are the potter:
> we are all the work of your hands.

Fr. Carey Landry has written "Abba Father," a beautiful song in which he suggests the logical conclusion to Isaiah's prayer: "Mold us, mold us and fashion us into the image of Jesus your son" (North American Liturgy Resources). Being molded and fashioned into the image of Jesus, becoming "other Christs," is precisely what Advent is all about: it is a program for Advent, indeed, for the entire Church year that lies ahead. All we have to do is to become good, malleable clay in the hands of God our Father, the Master Potter.

What is so remarkable about the image of the Father as a potter and us the clay is that it gives us a glimpse into the mystery mentioned above—the coming together of God's divine power, his grace, and our human freedom. God is Lord, Creator, all-powerful, all-knowing, but he stands helpless before a person who deliberately chooses not to allow him into that person's life. He can do nothing with us or for us unless we give full and free consent to be molded by him. We have to *want* him into our lives. And Advent gives us the chance to recognize that living our own life inevitably ends in failure and frustration: "We have all withered like leaves, and our guilt carries us away like the wind."

So . . . we can't be *forced* into serving our God, and we can't be *scared* either. Jesus is not trying to scare us when he tells us in the Gospel to be ready, to "be constantly on the watch" for his coming to us, either at the moment of death or the end of time. He wants us to make ourselves ready and *to desire* his coming into our lives now, wants us to want to be molded by the Father. He even gives us the right words to express our desire, our willingness to be molded: "To you, my God, I lift my soul, I trust in you; let me never come to shame" (Entrance Antiphon). And "Lord, make us turn to you, let us see your face and we shall be saved" (Responsorial Psalm).

That's the whole secret: we can't be forced; we have to choose freely, and the only thing that can make us want to choose to be molded by him is to see how beautiful, wonderful, and desirable is our God made flesh in Christ Jesus, the celebration of whose birth we look forward to with such anxiety. And so we pray:

> Father in heaven,
> our hearts desire the warmth of your love
> and our minds are searching for the light of your Word.
> Increase our longing for Christ our Savior
> and give us the strength to grow in love . . . .
> (Alternative Opening Prayer)

* * *

"Yet, O Lord, you are our father;
we are the clay and you are the potter;
we are all the work of your hands" *(Reading I).*

"Lord, make us turn to you, let us see your face and we shall be saved" *(Responsorial Psalm).*

"The Lord will shower his gifts, and our land will yield its fruit" *(Communion Antiphon).*

16

FIRST SUNDAY OF ADVENT   Cycle C

READING I	**Jer 33:14-16**	**READING II 1 Thess 3:12–4:2**
GOSPEL	**Luke 21:25-28, 34-36**	

Reading I: Christians believe that Jeremiah's prophecy that God will raise up for David a "just shoot" has been fulfilled in Jesus Christ.

Reading II: Paul tells the Thessalonians that the best way for them to prepare for the coming of Jesus at the end of time is by loving one another.

Gospel: Luke reports Jesus' prophecy about his Second Coming and warns his hearers to be on their guard, for they know not the hour of his coming.

The chief theme of today's Mass is the Second Coming of Christ at the end of time, and we recall that this was also the theme of the last Sundays of the year. So Advent doesn't just burst suddenly upon us.

Life comes and is lived in stages, each of which seems very brief, especially when you look back on it. All of a sudden you are an adolescent, then a young person beginning a career, then you are middle-aged and, seemingly the most sudden of all, you are old and you start wondering how it ever happened to you and how many years you have left to finish your work. You begin to believe that you are really going to die after all, and you may even start speculating on what life will be like in the world to come.

The story or history of the world and of humankind is the same, although the stages are obviously much longer. But one thing is certain: the end is inevitably coming, and it is the Lord himself (the one that started the whole process) who tells us so. And that message is the chief emphasis of the readings of the First Sunday of Advent in each cycle.

The Gospels of Matthew, Mark, and Luke all record our Lord's prophecies about the coming of the "end time"; but recording the collective community's at times confused memories of Jesus' sayings as they do, the evangelists sometimes mixed Jesus' prophecies about the end of the world with those of the coming destruction of Jerusalem and its glorious Temple. But there is one element that is common to each evangelist: it is that since we do not know when the Lord is coming or when death will come to us, it behooves us to be prepared. Thus today Jesus tells us: "The day I speak of will come upon all who dwell on the face of the earth, so be on the watch. . . . Pray constantly for the strength to escape whatever is in prospect, and to stand secure before the Son of Man" (Gospel).

The consciousness of the tradition of Christ's Second Coming was very strong among the first generations of Christians, and St. Paul both records and encourages it. But most of all he seeks to prepare his different communities for the inevitable. Today's message to the Thessalonians is typical: "May the Lord increase you and make you overflow with love for one another and for all . . . . May he strengthen your hearts, making them blameless and holy before our God . . . ."

Paul was wise both in divine wisdom and human psychology. He wanted the people to be prepared, but he didn't try to scare them, and he certainly didn't preach "hellfire and damnation." He simply told them that the best, the only way, to prepare was by allowing themselves to be possessed by love—for God and one another.

There is something else Paul would have wanted in them, an element he himself possessed in great degree, namely, a strong desire for eternal union of love with Christ. He often mentioned his wish to be dissolved and be with Christ. He would surely approve of both our Opening Prayers today:

> Increase our longing for Christ our Savior
> and give us the strength to grow in love . . . .
> (Alternative Opening Prayer)
> . . . increase our strength of will for doing good
> that Christ may find an eager welcome at his coming
> and call us to his side in the kingdom of heaven . . . .
> (Opening Prayer)

Another prominent theme stands out in today's Mass: our preparation this year for our celebration of the birth of Jesus and what that birth has to mean in terms of our present life. Just as physical life has its age-stages, so too our spiritual life has its stages. We grow hot and cold. Our love relationship with Christ is often like that of any married couple: love can diminish and wane. Advent is a time of renewal, of refreshment of our love-life with Christ . . . possibly even of rescue. Every Advent is new and different for us because we are new and different from one year to another. In our growth in love referred to in that Opening Prayer, we never remain on the same level—or we should not. If we do not grow in love, it can fade and we run the risk of losing it altogether.

So it is natural for us to look forward to a special spiritual renewal leading to a deeper love-encounter with Jesus at Christmas. We readily admit that the work of spiritual renewal in our lives and hearts is primarily the task of divine grace and that increase is the object of our prayer today:

Increase our longing for Christ our Savior . . . .
(Alternative Opening Prayer)

. . . increase our strength of will for doing good
that Christ may find an eager welcome at his coming . . . .
(Opening Prayer)

and

Your ways, O Lord, make known to me;
    teach me your paths.
Guide me in your truth and teach me,
    for you are God my savior,
and for you I wait all the day (Responsorial Psalm).

And our part? "To you, my God, I lift my soul, I trust in you; let me never come to shame. . . . No one who waits for you is ever put to shame" (Entrance Antiphon). To lift up our souls to God, full of hope, desire, expectancy, can be exciting, even thrilling. But we may want to be careful. He may even make us saints!

Lord, let us see your kindness,
and grant us your salvation (Gospel Verse).

* * *

"To you, my God, I lift my soul, I trust in you; let me never come to shame" *(Entrance Antiphon).*

"May the Lord increase you and make you overflow with love . . . ." *(Reading II).*

"The Lord will shower his gifts, and our land will yield its fruit" *(Communion Antiphon).*

READING I Isa 2:1-5
GOSPEL Matt 8:5-11

Reading I: Isaiah tells of a vision of the end times when the Lord's house will finally be established, and all peoples will gladly find their home in it.

Gospel: Jesus willingly consents to heal the paralyzed servant of a centurion. His eagerness to heal is matched by his delight at the centurion's deep faith.

Nations, hear the message of the Lord . . . : Our Savior is coming. Have no more fear (Entrance Antiphon).

Advent is longing, it is anticipation, it is hope. Above all, it is a cry for help and healing out of the very heart of humankind. And each of us who has any kind of worry or sorrow (Does that leave anybody out?) has a part in the longing. Advent is for now, it is for us in this living, hurting present. Come to us, Lord, and bring us peace.

Advent is for all mankind, but it is for each of us personally; it is for every family, every parish, every religious community. The wounds of sin, as well as the ravages of the human condition cry out with the centurion of today's Gospel: "Sir, my serving boy is at home in bed paralyzed, suffering painfully."

There is hardly a Gospel that more perfectly dramatizes our human condition, and there couldn't be a better choice for this beginning of Advent. The serving boy lying paralyzed in bed is all mankind; he is every family, he is you and I. The paralysis may be physical or mental or moral. It may be an evil habit; it may be envy, hatred, a refusal to forgive; or it may be poverty, loss of job, worry about a loved one. "Come and save us, Lord our God; let us see your face, and we shall be saved" (Gospel Verse).

And how does Jesus answer? Without hesitation he says, "I will come and cure him." As simple as that. But what will the cure consist in and when will it come? The cure may be somewhat disappointing if we conceive of it as a sudden miraculous lifting of all anxiety, pain, worry, agony. As long as we live in this world, we shall suffer in some manner or other, and at the end of our life we shall die.

So what will Jesus do for us? *He can (and will, if we really desire it) enable us to come to terms with life as it is, with all its griefs and joys.* And not just come to terms with life as it is in a negative kind of way, like "offering it up," but to give life, our life, a new meaning and value. Actually, to give it joy. The Communion Antiphon hints at this value: "Come to us, Lord, and bring us peace. We will rejoice in your presence and serve you with all our heart." At least five times the words "joy" or "joyful" are mentioned in this Mass. It seems it is possible to be joyous even when we suffer. To show us how to achieve this marvellous condition might well be the greatest of Advent's gifts to us. "Everyone must suffer both from oneself and from others, but the mark of whether it is Christian or not is the mark of joy and peace" (Edward Farrell: *Surprised by the Spirit* Denville, N.J.: Dimension Books, 1973, 47).

The Father knows us better than we know ourselves. He knows our weaknesses, he knows wounds that we are not aware of, even dimly. He helps us to recognize our wounds, our hurts. May he also help us to know the causes of these wounds, for we cannot be cured by Jesus unless we are willing to avoid these causes and so grow daily more and more in his image.

Lord our God,
help us to prepare
for the coming of Christ your Son.
May he find us waiting,
eager in joyous prayer.

Come, Lord Jesus!

* * *

"I rejoiced when I heard them say:
let us go to the house of the Lord" *(Responsorial Psalm)*.

"He [Jesus] said to him: 'I will come and cure him'" *(Gospel)*.

"Come to us, Lord, and bring us peace. We will rejoice in your presence and serve you with all our heart" *(Communion Antiphon)*.

177 TUESDAY OF THE FIRST WEEK OF ADVENT

READING I   Isa 11:1-10
GOSPEL   Luke 10:21-24

Reading I: We listen to Isaiah's prophecy of the blessed endowments of the Messiah to come and of the glorious messianic times that will arrive after his work and the work of his Church is finally accomplished.

Gospel: We hear the claim of Jesus that by his words and deeds he fulfills the ancient prophecies: "Blest are the eyes that see what you see."

The Lord is just; he will award the crown of justice to all who have longed for his coming (Communion Antiphon).

God alone could have had a vision of such beauty, fullness of promise and blessedness as the prophecy of the coming Messiah in Reading I. It is one of the loveliest of all Old Testament prophecies. The Messiah to come is of the line of Jesse, father of David; on him the Spirit of the Lord will come to rest—a spirit of wisdom and of understanding, a spirit of counsel and of strength, a spirit of knowledge and of fear of the Lord.

This first part of the prophecy is fulfilled in Jesus, as he himself claims, when in the Gospel he tells us: "Blest are the eyes that see what you see. I tell you, many prophets and kings wished to see what you see but did not see it, and to hear what you hear but did not hear it." Praise God, we are among those Jesus has in mind!

But then comes the second part of Reading I with its prophetic vision of a time when all ancient antagonisms and alienations between peoples, between people and beasts, people and nature will disappear, and a glorious harmony, unknown to humankind since the first entrance of evil into the world will again reign. These are the so-called messianic or end times, which are as much an object of Advent longing as deliverance from sin and the desire for peace and joy which are so much closer to our hearts' desire. The Responsorial Psalm echoes the prophecy: "Justice shall flourish in his time, and fullness of peace for ever."

Despite all the beauty of the end times, most modern Christians are understandably reluctant to wait that long for relief from present problems and anxieties. We need help *now*. Our prayer now is:

God of mercy and consolation,
help us in our weakness and free us from sin.
Hear our prayers
that we may rejoice at the coming of your Son . . . .
(Opening Prayer)

Do you know what we really need? What would be the best possible answer to our prayer? It would be for Jesus to share with us those gifts of the Holy Spirit that he possesses in such abundance (and which he will surely give us if we want them badly enough): the gift of WISDOM (an insight into the meaning of life and into the way the Lord has guided our personal life-development); the gift of UNDERSTANDING (grasping with mind and heart the power of Jesus in our lives); the gift of COUNSEL (the ability to discern God's ways in our lives and to help others towards that same discernment—a sense of consciousness of who we are and who others are and of how God is present to us and we to him); the gift of COURAGE or strength (the fearlessness that enables us to persevere despite all obstacles along a permanent path of commitment to Christ and his way of life); the gift of KNOWLEDGE (not just possessing facts but the experience of truth like that of Paul when he said, "I know him in whom I believe"; a knowledge of mind and heart, knowledge shot through with love); and the gift of the FEAR OF THE LORD (not terror or slavish fear, but a blessed, reverent sense of awe in the presence of divine Love in itself and, above all, divine love made flesh in Jesus our beloved Lord).

> Behold, our Lord will come with power,
> he will enlighten the eyes of his servants (Gospel Verse).

Hopefully, now we understand a little better what it is that we look forward to and long for with such demanding desire. I have never been able to get excited about desiring the end times . . . or even heaven when all sorrows will vanish. All that seems so far off. But why quibble? Isn't all desire desire for Christ? And that hunger for Christ is what we beg the Lord to increase and sharpen in us all.

But considering life as it is—with all its mystery, its pain, worry and agony—I see now that the deepest desire and need of our lives is an outpouring at Christmas, during Lent, at Easter and, above all, at Pentecost of these gifts of the Holy Spirit that God promised to pour out upon Jesus, his Son. He promised those gifts to him, not for him alone, but so that he might share them with us, his brothers and sisters. We believe in God's promise:

> He shall rescue the poor man when he cries out,
> and the afflicted when he has no one to help him.
> He shall have pity for the lowly and the poor;
> the lives of the poor he shall save (Responsorial Psalm).

This is the Father's promise. He keeps promises. Come, Lord Jesus!

* * *

"See, the Lord is coming and with him all his saints. Then there will be endless day" *(Entrance Antiphon).*

"Justice shall flourish in his time,
and fullness of peace for ever *(Responsorial Psalm).*

"Blest are the eyes that see what you see" *(Gospel).*

178 WEDNESDAY OF THE FIRST WEEK OF ADVENT

READING I   Isa 25:6-10
GOSPEL   Matt 15:29-37

Reading I: We enjoy Isaiah's vision of the eternal joys of heaven when all human hungers will be satisfied, and the Lord God will wipe away the tears from all faces.

Gospel: Jesus heals crowds of cripples and deformed and then feeds them miraculously with seven loaves and a few fishes.

The Lord is my shepherd; I shall not want.
In verdant pastures he gives me repose . . . . (Responsorial Psalm).

Hunger and the food that satisfies hunger provides the dominant theme of today's Mass. In the Opening Prayer we ask God to make us ready to share in the banquet of heaven, and Isaiah gives some idea of the joys of that longed-for banquet. We do not know the nature of the food that is being served in heaven, but since most people there do not have bodies (at least for the present) as we have, it hardly seems possible that they are consuming meat, potatoes, and vegetables. Nevertheless, Scripture has always used the symbolism of a banquet, "a feast of rich food and choice wines" (Reading I), to illustrate the joys and desirability of heaven.

That may come as a disappointment to the kind of Christian who thinks of food as a necessary evil and who entirely disapproves of wine. Couldn't the Lord have chosen a symbol more in keeping with our spiritual nature? Well, it's rather hard to argue with the One who created us according to his own plan. The Hebrews who composed Scripture under the inspiration of the Holy Spirit never did conceive of the human person as a kind of

24

split being, composed of body and soul. Man/woman was one, a single entity, a unified person; and this unified person had very deep needs—the need for material food to sustain life and, above all, the need for the spiritual food of God's word and sacrament to sustain his or her intimate relationship with Jesus. A human being hungers for God, and that hunger for material food and drink can very well be the best possible sign of that deepest of all hungers.

The beautiful symbolism of natural food does not, however, indicate that it is not without its dangers. To overindulge in food or drink not only makes one sick; it may well cause overweight, which, in turn, may require a diet. And dieting isn't much fun for anybody. But there is no danger of overindulging in the rich food of the divine word and the grace-giving sacraments, especially the Eucharist that nourishes the whole person. There are no problems of overweight in heaven, no calorie counting, and thank God, no dieting.

Well, this all provides an introduction to today's readings and texts. The banquet of rich food and choice wines points to the ultimate satisfaction for the deep hunger for God and for lasting happiness that drives us all our lives. There may well be considerable comfort for us in the vision of Isaiah in which our divine Host will not only gratify our hunger for him but also our hunger for a binding love that will destroy all enmities, when he "will wipe away the tears from all faces." On that day it will be said:

Behold our God, to whom we looked to save us!
This is the Lord for whom we looked;
let us rejoice and be glad that he has saved us!

It is in the light of this divine pedagogy on the nature of heaven that we can best grasp the deep meaning of Jesus' miraculous multiplication of the loaves and fishes. The first thing to be noted about the Gospel is that the miraculous multiplication followed the cure of crowds of deformed cripples and other unfortunates. And Jesus introduces the miracle with the revealing words: "My heart is moved with pity for the crowd. . . . I do not wish to send them away hungry, for fear they may collapse on the way."

That day Jesus saw before him more than a Palestinian crowd: his vision went out into all future times; it included unfortunates of every land, it included us. "My heart is moved with pity for the crowd." That day he fed the people with bread and fish. Now he feeds us with himself, his body and blood and his word. He gives us the fulfillment of what the miracle points to—the Eucharist, and so he provides us with a foretaste of the heavenly banquet foretold by Isaiah. The prayer of the psalmist is now our prayer:

Even though I walk in the dark valley
    I fear no evil; for you are at my side
With your rod and your staff
    that give me courage (Responsorial Psalm).

* * *

"Behold our God, to whom we looked to save us!" *(Reading I)*.

"My heart is moved with pity for the crowd" *(Gospel)*.

"Only goodness and kindness follow me
all the days of my life . . . ." *(Responsorial Psalm)*.

179 THURSDAY OF THE FIRST WEEK OF ADVENT

READING I   Isa 26:1-6
GOSPEL   Matt 7:21, 24-27

Reading I: Isaiah asks God to open up the walls of his city for "a nation
that is just, one that keeps faith," and he pleads with his people to trust in the Lord forever.

Gospel: Religion does not consist in pious words, but in doing the will
of the Father. Trust in the Lord is the only solid foundation
for the house of our faith.

It is better to take refuge in the Lord
    than to trust in princes (Responsorial Psalm).

In today's prayer we cry out:

Father,
we need your help.
Free us from sin and bring us to life.
Support us by your power.

"We need your help" is a considerable understatement, and each
of us can personally identify the help needed. The Church con-
siders it important to specify freedom from sin (which can be a living death), together with restoration to life, and for good measure
she asks the Father to support us by and with his power.

I would like to suggest that the real help, the genuine divine power we need most of all is the power to trust in our loving Father and in his promises to us. "Trust in the Lord forever," Isaiah counsels us in Reading I, "for the Lord is an eternal rock." The psalmist adds:

> It is better to take refuge in the Lord
> than to trust in man

—another understatement.

To take refuge in the Lord is very descriptive of what trust really is. It is realizing that we are safe with him. But trust in the Lord is more than reliance on God and seeking security in his arms. Trust in God is possible for us *because God first trusts us.* Although we so often let him down, he never loses confidence in us, never gives up on us. Fr. John Shea tells us that trust implies "an active empowerment of others to be everything they can be . . . to trust someone is to call him to his better self, to act in a new way" *(The Challenge of Jesus.* Chicago: Thomas More Press, 1975, 130).

Is not this what the Father desires for all of us as a result of our celebration of Advent this year? He calls us to our better self, and if we desire that as much as he does, he will grant it and will "empower us to live creatively in an unmanageable existence" (Shea, 133).

> Seek the Lord while he can be found.
> Call on him while he is near (Gospel Verse).

Trust in our Father, in response to his trust in us, is also what Jesus recommends in the Gospel. Happiness in the world to come and a sense of self-assurance in this world do not result from mouthing pious words or divine names, but from "doing the will of the Father in heaven." And isn't that just another way of saying that salvation comes from trusting in the Father's love?

Jesus goes on to draw up plans for the construction of our personal house of faith. Just as a man with any sense will build his house on a solid, reliable foundation rather than on sand, so the wise Christian will seek out a solid foundation for his house of faith. "Anyone who hears my words and puts them into practice is like the wise man who built his house on rock." Is it possible to find a more solid foundation than trust in the Father? Was not this the way that Jesus himself followed?

We need divine help, and God knows our greatest need: trust in him. May we come to know in our hearts how much he has trusted in us in the past, but, above all, help us to respond to that trust and so to live creatively in this present difficult life of ours.

* * *

"Trust in the Lord forever! For the Lord is an eternal rock" *(Reading I)*.

"Seek the Lord while he can be found.
Call on him while he is near" *(Gospel Verse)*.

"Blessed is he who comes in the name of the Lord;
we bless you from the house of the Lord" *(Responsorial Psalm)*.

180   FRIDAY OF THE FIRST WEEK OF ADVENT

READING I   Isa 29:17-24
GOSPEL   Matt 9:27-31

Reading I: Isaiah has a vision of messianic times when the deaf will hear, the blind will see, and "the lowly will ever find joy in the Lord . . . ."

Gospel: Jesus heals two blind men who cry out to him, "Son of David, have pity on us." "Because of your faith, it shall be done to you . . . ."

Behold, our Lord shall come with power,
he will enlighten the eyes of his servants. Alleluia (Gospel Verse).

The gift of sight is appreciated most when it is threatened or lost. The loss of sight can be devastating for a person, especially for one who has an appreciative eye for beauty in nature or in people. All the world's blind can make their own cry of the two blind men in today's Gospel, "Son of David, have pity on us!"

There are, of course, various kinds of blindness. The inability to behold the world around us, with its limitless treasury of delights, is a frightful deprivation. It means that one of the most essential avenues of God's goodness, beauty, and grace into our inmost being is closed off, and that in turn means that he has to find other avenues—for him no very great problem. The avenue he most wishes to use is the touch of the hand of a loving friend, the sound of a caring voice, the song of birds, or the inspired music of a choir or an orchestra. Blind people are often happier and holier than those who can see, but fail to respond to the glory they behold.

Devastating though physical blindness is, it cannot compare with blindness of heart in all its variations. The person whose mind and heart are not lifted up at the view of a beautiful sunrise or sunset is a sadly deprived being. But even worse off is the one who is unable to perceive the devastation of lovelessness or indifference in his or her life or the person who refuses to see sorrow and need and neglect in those around him.

"Son of David, have pity on us!" We all, to some degree, are blind in one way or another. The cry of the blind men of the Gospel is our cry, our Advent plea for vision, for the perfecting of the vision of our minds, our hearts, our understanding of the mystery of life, of suffering, yes, even of the mystery of evil in all its manifestations. "We are waiting for our Savior, the Lord Jesus Christ; he will transfigure our lowly bodies into copies of his own glorious body" (Communion Antiphon).

Actually, the Lord our God promises us such a vision. The picture painted in Reading I is of messianic times, as is the Communion Antiphon just quoted, but maybe our earnest pleading can hasten or anticipate those times a little:

On that day the deaf shall hear
  the words of a book;
And out of gloom and darkness,
  the eyes of the blind shall see.
The lowly will ever find joy in the Lord,
  and the poor rejoice in the Holy One of Israel (Reading I).

"Son of David, have pity on us! So the promise is there, and also the assurance of Jesus. But it seems that he needs more from us than the basic cry for help. He addresses us now, as he spoke to the blind men then: "Are you confident I can do this?" The blind men did not hesitate. "Yes, Lord," they cried. And Jesus touched their eyes and said, "Because of your faith it shall be done to you." And they recovered their sight.

* * *

"One thing I ask of the Lord;
  this I seek:
To dwell in the house of the Lord
  all the days of my life,
That I may gaze on the loveliness of the Lord
  and contemplate his temple" (Responsorial Psalm).

"Behold, our Lord shall come with power,
he will enlighten the eyes of his servants" (Gospel Verse).

"The Lord is coming from heaven in splendor to visit his people,
and bring them peace and eternal life" (Entrance Antiphon).

READING I   Isa 30:19-21, 23-26
GOSPEL   Matt 9:35–10:1, 6-8

Reading I: We have another promise of the happiness of messianic times. The Lord "will be gracious to you when you cry out, as soon as he hears he will answer you."

Gospel: Moved with pity at the crowds of sick people, Jesus commissions his disciples to take up and carry on his own work of healing and comforting.

Come, Lord, from your cherubim throne; let us see your face, and we shall be saved (Entrance Antiphon).

Today's Mass marvellously illustrates one of the extraordinary features of the Advent liturgy: we plead for the coming of the Son of God when in actual fact he has already come, we already have him, as the Opening Prayer states:

God our Father,
you loved the world so much
you gave your only Son to free us
from the ancient power of sin and death.
Help us who wait for his coming,
and lead us to true liberty.

As Fr. Adrian Nocent, O.S.B., puts it, "The Christian hopes for what he already possesses" (*The Liturgical Year* [Advent]. Collegeville, Minn.: The Liturgical Press, 1977, 30).

And that's perfectly all right. We never cease needing Jesus and his healing, compassionate touch. "At the sight of the crowds, his heart was moved with pity," today's Gospel tells us. Is there any reason to believe that his pity and compassion ceased with the termination of his life in Palestine long ago? I believe that his pity is everlasting and is just as effective now as it was then. How true of Jesus are the words of the Responsorial Psalm:

He heals the brokenhearted
and binds up their wounds.
He tells the number of the stars;
he calls each by name.

It is no accident that the psalmist sees those two ideas as related. The Son of God, God before all ages, Lord of the planets and stars, will continue healing the brokenhearted till time itself ends. But how does he do the healing now? The Gospel tells us that he summoned his twelve disciples and gave them authority to expel unclean spirits and to cure sickness and disease of every kind:

"Cure the sick, raise the dead, heal the leprous, expell demons. The gift you have received, give as a gift." That commission has never been withdrawn from the Church, and her members, especially those in charge, may never forget it. As long as there are human persons anywhere "lying prostrate from exhaustion, like sheep without a shepherd," the Church has her Christlike work cut out for her. And we are the Church, you and I.

But the Church has another, equally important task to do for her children. It is that *of celebrating and making present again here and now* the original birth, life, and death of her Savior. We celebrate that coming at every Mass, but in some mysterious and wonderful way, we are also looking forward to the Savior's birth in our midst at Christmas. "Come, Lord, from your cherubim throne . . . ." (Entrance Antiphon) "Happy are all who long for the coming of the Lord" (Responsorial Psalm). And how does our God answer our plea for his coming? In the Communion Antiphon he promises, "I am coming quickly, says the Lord, and will repay each man according to his deeds." That sounds more like a threat than it really is. Knowing Jesus as we do from the Gospels, he's not the type who seeks revenge for evil deeds. He loves sinners and pleads for them to come back to him. This is why we pray in the Communion Prayer:

> God of mercy,
> may this eucharist bring us your divine help,
> free us from our sins,
> and prepare us for the birthday of our Savior . . . .

> Great is our Lord and mighty in power:
> to his wisdom there is no limit (Responsorial Psalm).

Through the mouth of his prophet Isaiah, the Father in today's Reading I promises us the bread we need and the water for which we thirst. And then he says something extremely significant: "A voice shall sound in your ears: 'This is the way; walk in it. . . .'" I wonder if this is not what Fr. John Shea had in mind when he wrote of Jesus: "He is the entrance into the religious reality of the Father, into the depths of God, self, neighbor relationship. It must be stressed that Jesus is a way into the mystery of human existence and not a way out of current problems" (*The Challenge of Jesus.* Chicago: Thomas More Press, 1975, 47).

I like that idea very much, but I wonder if we have to be exclusive. God is our Father, we are his children, and we need help. His Son Jesus told us to remind him of our needs; so again we remind him that he is our greatest need. Come, Lord Jesus!

* * *

"Come, Lord, from your cherubim throne; let us see your face, and we shall be saved" *(Entrance Antiphon)*.

"Happy are all who long for the coming of the Lord" *(Responsorial Psalm)*.

"The gift you have received, give as a gift" *(Gospel)*.

4 SECOND SUNDAY OF ADVENT Cycle A

READING I Isa 11:1-10 **READING II** Rom 15:4-9
GOSPEL Matt 3:1-12

Reading I: Isaiah foresees the coming of a Messiah of the line of David who will be filled with the spirit of the Lord.

Reading II: Paul tells the Romans that Scripture was written for their instruction and also to provide them with hope.

Gospel: We meet John the Baptizer who tells us to prepare the way of the Lord, to make straight his paths.

In Reading II St. Paul gives us a valuable lesson on how to understand the ideas of Isaiah and other Old Testament prophets we hear during Advent: "Everything written before our time was written for our instruction, that we might derive hope from the lessons of patience and the words of encouragement in the Scriptures."

Today Isaiah describes the coming Messiah as one who comes from the Jesse-David line, one who will be filled with the spirit of the Lord—the spirit of wisdom, understanding, counsel, strength, a spirit of knowledge and of fear of the Lord. Isaiah also provides a hint of conditions that will prevail at the end of time (a prominent Advent theme): peace will reign between all creatures, human and animal, and between humankind and nature—all goals towards which we all struggle and labor from year to year.

Today in the Gospel we renew acquaintance with an old, but uncomfortable, friend. His name is John the Baptist, and he's been with us a long time. At regular intervals he reenters our lives, and we are never quite the same afterwards. His message to us is all too familiar: "Reform your lives! The reign of God is at hand." He is "A herald's voice in the desert: 'Prepare the way of the Lord, make straight his paths.'"

We should be able to understand such language. Take a look at the highway map of the United States. You can get on Interstate 35 in Duluth and drive straight south to the Mexican border. When a superhighway is built, the contractors make every effort to remove sharp curves; they fill in depressions, cut through hills and mountains so that the way to the destination can be traveled most directly.

John never saw a superhighway, but he uses the image in order to prepare the way for the coming of the world's most wonderful and extraordinary traveler, the Messiah Jesus, into our lives. The highway John wishes to construct is within our hearts. It hasn't a number, but it does have a name—*conversion.*

John's message now is not primarily to Jews, nor to pagans, but to us who call ourselves Christians. When Archbishop Joseph Bernardin was president of the conference of American bishops, he said to his fellow bishops at a meeting: "Catholics cannot evangelize the eighty million unchurched in the United States when so many Catholics themselves have yet to experience conversion."

For the Pharisee named Saul, conversion took place in a moment. So too the conversion of the great English religious writer C. S. Lewis. He tells of driving to the zoo. "When we set out I did not believe that Jesus Christ is the Son of God, and when we reached the zoo I did. Yet I had not spent the journey in thought. Nor in great emotion."

For most of us Christians, however, conversion is the work of a lifetime, and each of us experiences it in his or her own way. What really is conversion? If we have ever looked closely into our inmost heart, we might get the uneasy feeling that we are not quite complete, not quite whole; we might see that some desirable Christlike attitude or quality is missing, that our inner life is too scattered, not centered on Jesus, or that there is a discrepancy between the kind of person we are now and the kind of person we can become and know we ought to become. Conversion builds on the recognition of this lack of unity and completeness in our life.

So we can make two points about conversion: *1.* The call to conversion is a summons to become the fully developed human person each of us is capable of becoming; *2.* Conversion responds to a human need for wholeness. We experience the continuing necessity to pull together the scattered pieces of our lives. But any pagan can do this. It's simply an effort to become more human. Is there anything specifically Christian about conversion? We know, of course, that it is Jesus. That's what it was for Saul for whom Jesus became the primary and exclusive preoccupation. In Jesus we see the breadth and depth of what it means to be whole, to be a complete human being. In him we see what our own life is called to be. Conversion results when a person realizes profoundly that the message and life of Jesus of Nazareth makes sense and is infinitely desirable.

> God of power and mercy,
> open our hearts in welcome.
> Remove the things that hinder us from receiving Christ with
> joy . . . . (Opening Prayer).

Conversion takes place when Jesus and his message cut through the moments of pain, tears, worry, fear, and uneasiness in our lives; he pulls us together and makes us conscious at long last that he alone matters. Conversion means meeting Jesus in his word and allowing him to become directly involved in our lives. He and we become related in a personal and marvellous way, so that he becomes as real to us as our closest and best friend.

Once this happens, life can never again be the same for us. We answer the summons to reexamine and possibly change the values of our lives—the ideas, the ideals, the customary habits of thought that we consider essential. Habits of thought, convictions, that do not stand the test of the Gospel no longer remain the be-all and end-all of life. Christ and he alone fulfills that purpose. We live under him, we live for him, by him and with him, and not only with him but with our neighbor as well. Loving concern for all persons replaces callousness, indifference, neglect, dislike.

This is the message of John the Baptist for us today . . . as it was then and always will be. But Advent is more than a negative time for rooting out character defects and weaknesses. It is a time for positive growth—for bringing forth fruits of honesty, neighborly concern, Christ-like generosity, unselfish love. Our Christian faith imposes responsibility upon us: to take it for granted, as the Pharisees seemed to do with their religious practice, is one evil; to think we can live it out alone, by our own power, without help from Jesus and others is another. That is why we need the sacraments, especially the Eucharist and the sacrament of reconciliation (Penance). We should start now to prepare ourselves for our Advent confession, with the words of John ringing in our ears and hearts: "Reform your lives! The reign of God is at hand. . . . Prepare the way of the Lord, make straight his paths." Come, Lord Jesus!

* * *

"Justice shall flourish in his time, and fullness of peace for ever"
(Responsorial Psalm).

34

READING I   Isa 40:1-5; 9-11   READING II   2 Pet 3:8-14
GOSPEL   Mark 1:1-8

Reading I: God tells Isaiah to comfort his people, but again asks them to prepare the way of the Lord and make straight a highway for his coming.

Reading II: Like Paul, Peter believes that Christ will come again soon, when least expected, and therefore all should be prepared.

Gospel: Mark opens his Gospel with the picture of John proclaiming the need for all to repent and be baptized so as to be ready to receive the Messiah into their lives.

As we listen to John's very stern and imperious summons to repent and be converted, it is terribly important for us to see this summons in the context of the idea of God given to us today by Isaiah. Knowing his people's pains better than they do themselves, God tells Isaiah:

Comfort, give comfort to my people . . . .
Speak tenderly to Jerusalem, and proclaim to her
    that her service is at an end . . . .

Salvation will come, for he loves and forgives his people:

Like a shepherd he feeds his flock;
    in his arms he gathers the lambs,
Carrying them in his bosom . . . .

That's the kind of God *we* have. Not terrifying and fearsome, but tender, kind, forgiving, loving.

Peter, the chief shepherd of the flock entrusted to him by Christ, tells his people that the best way to prepare for the coming of the Lord is to be ''holy in your conduct and devotion, looking for the coming of the day of God and trying to hasten it!'' ''He shows you generous patience, since he wants none to perish but all to come to repentance.''

''Lord, let us see your kindness, and grant us your salvation'' (Responsorial Psalm).

The message of Advent can never change or be changed: Prepare the way for the Lord, make his paths straight. The very preparation can bring us closer to God, especially if we go about it seriously. All the readings today speak to real life-situations: for the Jews in captivity in Babylon; for the early Christian community which was longing for the Second Coming of Christ and being

35

threatened by persecution for their faith; for the people of Jesus' time who did not yet know him and were listening to his precursor John the Baptizer.

All were troubled with a variety of problems, all needed deliverance, all needed a Messiah-Savior. But the kind of Messiah God sent in the fullness of time was not necessarily the one they thought they should have. This was above all the case with Christ and his contemporaries who were under the domination of the Roman emperor.

We may not be in exile as the Jews were in Babylon, and we surely are not persecuted as the first Christians were. But who of us does not have worries and concerns, either personal or involving those we love. We have to think of others. What must be the pain, the worry, the distress of so many people whose hopes are gradually being crushed by rising prices, inflation, job insecurity—to say nothing of their family trials and anxieties! People need help, they need hope, they need comfort and rescue at so many levels of life.

Christ the Savior did not while he lived and does not now provide relief from inflation or any other kind of threat any more than he provided political rescue for his contemporaries. Not that he is unconcerned about the personal problems that afflict every person alive. Actually, he suffers with us. What he does promise and provide is some kind of understanding, of meaning, for life: he allows us to join our sufferings to his own for the greater good of the world, and he provides courage and strength to come to terms with life and suffering.

But we have to prepare. Advent is always a new beginning. Mark's Gospel is a good beginning for any Advent. He starts: "Here begins the gospel of Jesus Christ, the Son of God." It is as though he were saying to his readers then, several decades after Jesus had lived: "You people have been experiencing the saving power of Christ's death and resurrection. Do you want to know how it all began? These sixteen chapters will tell you." Advent is a new beginning aiming at a new creation in us and in the Church. But there has to be preparation, and the one to help us prepare for this new creation is John. Listen to him:

> Prepare the way for the Lord, make straight his paths:
> all mankind shall see the salvation of God (Gospel Verse).

John preaches repentance, *metanoia*, change, renewal, return to God. "Change yourselves from deep within," is the focus of his message. "Let the power of God invade your being and topple everything evil and make a new beginning in you. You will then be ready for the stronger one to come, he who will baptize you, cleanse you, with the power of the Holy Spirit."

> God of power and mercy,
> open our hearts in welcome.
> Remove the things that hinder us from receiving Christ with
> joy . . . . (Opening Prayer).

Our preparation is essentially an opening of our inner being to God's comforting and healing presence so that the Holy Spirit can transform and make a new creation of us. Repentance begins with recognizing our need for change and renewal, with dissatisfaction with who and what we are, and with the progress we have made in following Christ. This recognition of our unsatisfactory spiritual condition is basic to desire, and desire is what Advent preparation is all about. We recall last Sunday's prayer:

> Increase our longing for Christ our Savior
> and give us the strength to grow in love. . . .

Repentance is twofold: it is *negative*—that is, ridding ourselves of sins, weaknesses, imperfections of character and attitudes. But essentially it is *positive*—it is desire, longing, hope. It is prayer: deep, intense, fervent, loving—like the prayer of Mary, the Mother of Jesus. This coming Friday we will pray:

> May we live as he has taught,
> ready to welcome him with burning love and faith (Opening Prayer).

> "Lord, let us see your kindness, and grant us your salvation"
> (Responsorial Psalm).

Thus do we pray. And how will the Lord answer us?

> Here is your God! . . .
> Like a shepherd he feeds his flock;
> in his arms he gathers the lambs,
> Carrying them in his bosom,
> and leading the ewes with care.

Come, Lord Jesus!

* * *

"People of Zion, the Lord will come to save all nations, and your hearts will exult to hear his majestic voice" *(Entrance Antiphon)*.

"Kindness and truth shall meet; justice and peace shall kiss" *(Responsorial Psalm)*.

"Rise up, Jerusalem, stand on the heights, and see the joy that is coming to you from God" *(Communion Antiphon)*.

READING I   Bar 5:1-9   READING II   Phil 1:4-6, 8-11
GOSPEL   Luke 3:1-6

Reading I: The prophet Baruch has a vision of freedom for his exiled people when God will lead them back to Jerusalem in joy by the light of his glory.

Reading II: Paul writes tenderly to the Philippians, assuring them that what God begins in them in baptism he will bring to completion . . . if their love abounds more and more.

Gospel: Luke situates the familiar entrance of John the Baptist into human history at a specific time in the history of the Roman Empire and his own people.

> Up, Jerusalem! stand upon the heights;
>   look to the east and see your children
> Gathered from the east and the west
>   at the word of the Holy One . . . . (Reading I).

These words gave assurance and joy to the people in exile. They ought to mean even more to us, who have lived in the Christian era foretold in Baruch's vision. "The Lord has done great things for us; we are filled with joy" (Responsorial Psalm). But we can and should still "look to the east," to the rising sun, the Light of the world, symbol of Christ, whose birth we are to celebrate at Christmas. We can make ready the way for him into our hearts and lives by learning to value the things that really matter (Reading II).

The main theme of all three cycles of the Masses of the Second Sunday of Advent is John the Baptist's summons to repentance and conversion. He'll be returning with some specifics next Sunday. But knowing ourselves as we do, is there any *hope* for our conversion? If there isn't, conversion will not take place. And then Advent would be wasted so far as we are concerned.

Advent is supposed to be the time for hope. But how much do we know about this virtue? We hear a lot of sermons about love and faith, but how many do we ever hear about hope and our deep need for it? And yet, hope, along with faith and charity, is supposed to be the very foundation of our Christian religion.

The French poet Charles Péguy in his poem "Abandonment" puts the following words in God's mouth:

> I know how to handle man. It's my business. You can ask a lot of kindness of him, a lot of charity, a lot of sacrifice. But what you can't ask of him, by gum, is a little hope. A little confidence, don't you know, a little yielding, a little abandonment into my hands (*Basic Verities.* New York: Pantheon Books, 1943, 217).

We use the word hope a lot. Most often in a careless kind of way. We hope it won't rain or snow; we hope we'll hear from a loved one; we hope we'll keep our health or get well if we are ill. But none of this is authentic Christian hope.

What, then, is hope? It is closely allied to faith. In fact, it is said to be the "warmth and joy and dedication of faith" (*A New Catechism*, New York: Herder and Herder, 1967, 297–298).

> Hope is that aspect of faith which makes us certain that the world is cared for and loved by God. Hope is not vulgar optimism, not just looking on the sunny side of things and saying, "Let's hope for the best." *True hope is possible only if the ultimates in life give grounds for hope.* The grounds for Christian hope are God's eternity and Christ's resurrection, and also God's goodness—that he will not abandon us for whom Jesus lived, as long as we cling to him. Such confidence is not something which we can produce in ourselves. It is the gift of the Holy Spirit (*A New Catechism*, Italics added).

The Hebrew people lived in hope. They hoped for deliverance from their enemies, from oppression and persecution, in a word, they hoped for a Messiah, a Savior. The whole Old Testament, especially the prophets like Isaiah, is a book of hope, a book of promise. And in his Letter to the Romans, St. Paul expresses his prayer, his hope, that we might share in that Jewish hope, that by "the encouragement of the Scriptures we might have hope."

Many Jews still live in that hope . . . or have given its object a different meaning. Christians, on the other hand, believe that the hoped-for Messiah has come. The hope of the Jews has become the heart, the core, the very foundation of Christianity. It is also our consolation and joy.

Nevertheless, we still need hope, perhaps in our time more than ever. And hope isn't always easy to come by . . . or to rekindle, if we have lost it. Now, more than ever before in human history, we live in a threatened world. The press of fingers on a few buttons could destroy us all. Then there are the personal worries, concerns, and anguish that threaten our own happiness and that of our loved ones. Hope? How can we hope? What do we have to look forward to?

It is obvious that we shall have to reconcile ourselves to the recognition that we are never going to have any kind of idyllic existence in this life; we are never going to find a sorrowless, painless, worryless, deathless world. Our condition is human, it is fragile, and so shall it always be.

But we can hope for the discovery of some meaning in this life, the discovery that the simplest, most unexciting, most hidden, most apparently useless life counts—and that this world can be a better world.

Meaning for our life is precisely what the incarnation has provided and still provides if only we are willing to accept it. THE WORD WAS MADE FLESH. What does that mean? Much more than that he became flesh in Mary's womb. It means his making-himself-at-one with humankind, with us. It means his assuming *our* flesh, *our* weaknesses, even our sins. We are one with him and he is now one with us.

Therefore, it is this life of ours that counts now: this daily life of suffering, enduring, growing old, and approaching death. *This* is the flesh into which the Word has come . . . and still comes . . . still remains. This life here and now is the scene of the incarnation this year and every year . . . until he comes again. THE WORD WAS MADE FLESH. This is our grounds for hope. But the event has to be grasped with a living faith. And it has to be *celebrated,* and we'll take care of that at Christmas. God has been faithful to his promises. Out of love for us God has become man, flesh of our flesh. There *is* meaning in life. Our life belongs not only to us, but to Jesus . . . and to our world.

All this is as important to the young as to the old. All of us, young or old, have to communicate hope. Every one of us knows someone who lives without hope, who lives in constant dread of the future, overwhelmed by pessimism and even despair. Genuine hope, founded on the fact of Christ's birth, life, death, and resurrection, cannot be concealed. Like love it must manifest itself in the life, the attitudes, the quiet serenity of a personality that refuses to be crushed by the contagion of pessimism and despair. In a word, hope must communicate itself, manifest itself, if it is to endure. We can keep and grow in hope only if we are willing to share it. And isn't that the same with all the virtues—faith, hope, charity?

Péguy in his poem "Hope" puts these words in God's mouth:

I am, says God, the Lord of virtues.
Faith is a sanctuary lamp that burns forever.
Charity is that big, beautiful log fire
that you light in your hearth
so that my children the poor may come and warm themselves
before it on winter evenings.
And all around faith, I see all my faithful
kneeling together in the same attitude, and with one voice
uttering the same prayer.
And all around charity, I see all my poor
sitting in a circle around that fire,
And holding out their palms to the heat of the hearth.

But my hope is the bloom, and the fruit, and the leaf,
and the limb,
Hope is the shoot, and the bud of the bloom of
Eternity itself.

Men and Saints. New York: Pantheon Books, 1944, 249.

Advent is the time of hope. "Rise up, Jerusalem, stand on the heights, and see the joy that is coming to you from God" (Communion Antiphon).

* * *

"The Lord has done great things for us; we are filled with joy" *(Responsorial Psalm).*

"Prepare the way for the Lord, make straight his paths:
all mankind shall see the salvation of God" *(Gospel Verse).*

"For God will show all the earth your splendor:
 you will be named by God forever
 the peace of justice, the glory of God's worship. . . .
 For God is leading Israel in joy
 by the light of his glory,
 with his mercy and justice for company" *(Reading I).*

182 MONDAY OF THE SECOND WEEK OF ADVENT

READING I   Isa 35:1-10
GOSPEL   Luke 5:17-26

Reading I: The prophet pictures the "Messianic times" in the beautiful imagery of a rejoicing desert and a humanity healed of all its ills.

Gospel: We are present at the spiritual and physical healing of a paralytic. Jesus proves he can forgive sin by this miracle of healing.

The many themes of Advent coalesce and come together in today's Mass: longing for peace; wholeness and freedom from ourselves and our frailties; an awareness of our sinfulness—personal and communal; an assurance of forgiveness and the divine assurance that all our desires for fulfillment will be satisfied. "Nations, hear the message of the Lord, and make it known to the ends of the earth: Our Savior is coming. Have no more fear" (Entrance Antiphon).

We pray in the Opening Prayer for freedom from our sins and wholeness of mind and body:

Hear our prayer,
and prepare us to celebrate the incarnation of your Son . . . .

The prayer is an admission that sin enslaves us and diminishes us as persons. If we examine ourselves and look into our hearts, we hardly need proof of that statement.

Will our prayer be answered? In Reading I the Lord himself assures us that it will be. Isaiah uses imagery that should not be too difficult for us to understand, even if we do not live in or near a desert:

The desert and the parched land will exult;
the steppe will rejoice and bloom. . . .
They will see the glory of the Lord,
the splendor of our God (Reading I).

It's all so beautiful, but we who have heard it year after year may be allowed to wonder when it's all going to happen. To be sure, we are told that Isaiah envisions the "end times," the period of unthreatened peace and joy that will come after the end of the world as we know it. What we need and want is some help and assurance *now* in our sad present condition and in the years that remain of our lives. We seem to want heaven on earth right now. But how realistic is such a desire? Has *anyone* ever enjoyed a painless, anxiety-free existence in this life?

Well, what do we want then? Maybe a better question would be, "What do we need?" We need freedom from our various addictions to self-gratification (a fancy name for old-fashioned sin). We need a freshened vision of our life in relation to Christ's original coming and his coming again at Christmas. We need renewed confidence in Christ's unceasing presence to and in us *now*. We need courage, along with the assurance that our world will be a better world because of our having lived, suffered, and worked in it.

The assurance of our personal worth and the worthwhileness of our life will be one of the fruits of our forthcoming celebration of Christmas.

> Our God will come to save us!
> Kindness and truth shall meet;
>   justice and peace shall kiss. . . .
> The Lord himself will give his benefits. . . . (Responsorial Psalm).

But the real assurance we need is that we will be freed from our sins and made whole. And Jesus in the Gospel provides that assurance. What he did for the paralytic, he is more than willing to do for us. "My friend, your sins are forgiven you." But there are responsibilities of our own that we need to be concerned about as Advent progresses. We need to want to be lowered down through the roof of our indifference and defeatism to the feet of Jesus present to us in so many different ways, above all, in the sacraments of reconciliation and the Eucharist. In a word, we have to *want to be forgiven* and restored to greater intimacy with Christ. Nothing will happen to us at Christmas—the feast will be totally meaningless for us—without longing desire for a more conscious awareness of Christ Jesus in our lives.

We pray: "Come to us, Lord, and bring us peace. We will rejoice in your presence and serve you with all our heart" (Communion Antiphon). He says to us: "You come to me and you shall have peace. Then and only then will you really be able to rejoice in my presence and serve me with all your heart."

* * *

"Our Savior is coming. Have no more fear" *(Entrance Antiphon)*.

"Behold, the king will come, the Lord of earth:
and he will set us free" *(Gospel Verse)*.

"My friend, your sins are forgiven you" *(Gospel)*.

183 TUESDAY OF THE SECOND WEEK OF ADVENT

READING I   Isa 40:1-11
GOSPEL   Matt 18:12-14

Reading I: Isaiah comforts his people with the promise that God himself will come to save them; like a shepherd he will feed and carry his lambs in his bosom.

Gospel: The story of the man leaving ninety-nine sheep in the hills and going out in search of one that is lost tells about God's concern for each of us who strays from his loving care.

Jesus assures us today: "It is no part of your heavenly Father's plan that a single one of these little ones shall ever come to grief." He is talking about us. This is the conclusion to the story he tells us of the man who loses a single sheep and then, leaving the ninety-nine, goes off in search of the one stray. When he finds it, he is happier "than about the ninety-nine that did not wander away."

The practical realist might think that such solicitude about a single lost sheep is a little extreme, even a bit ridiculous. But Jesus assures us: he is not talking about real sheep. He's talking about us, you and me. Actually, he has in mind all humankind. What Jesus leaves unsaid in this story is the part he is to play in the real-life divine effort to recover the strayed sheep. He will reveal the details of his personal involvement in another parable, that of the Good Shepherd, which is to be found in John's Gospel, chapter 10: "I am the good shepherd; the good shepherd lays down his life for the sheep. . . . I know my sheep and my sheep know me . . . ." Jesus tells that parable after he fulfills all that is prophesied about him today.

Today's prophecy is marvellously expressive and heart-warming:

> Here comes with power
>   the Lord God . . .
> Here is his reward with him . . . .
> Like a shepherd he feeds his flock . . .
> Carrying them in his bosom,
>   and leading the ewes with care.

The Jerome Biblical Commentary tells us that "Isaiah reveals God as a shepherd-king, attracting, even carrying his people" (Englewood Cliffs, N.J.: Prentice-Hall, 1968, 369). We all know from personal experience that Jesus, the fulfillment of the prophecy, is much more satisfying than the prophecy itself.

Actually, the entire lesson is "love-talk," and the one who uses it is God himself, our Father:

Comfort, give comfort to my people . . . .
Speak tenderly to Jerusalem, and proclaim to her
  that her service is at an end,
  her guilt is expiated . . . .

The immediate object of this reassuring promise is God's people in exile in Babylon in the sixth century before Christ. They will return from exile to Jerusalem, and their homecoming will seem to them like the glory of the Lord shining over them. But the return and restoration involve some obligation on their part:

In the desert prepare the way of the Lord!
Make straight in the wasteland a highway for our God!

We know that the prophet is not talking about highway construction. But perhaps "highway repairs" might give some idea of the meaning the prophet has in mind. He is talking about our personal filling in of the potholes and leveling the dips in the road God wants to take into our inmost heart. He's talking about repentance for our having deliberately detoured from our God, about the roadblocks of selfishness and sin we have erected along that roadway. "The Lord is just; he will award the crown of justice to all who have longed for his coming" (Communion Antiphon).

So it seems there are four levels of God's comings and goings: the historical level in which the prophecy first applied, the level of the birth of Jesus we celebrate each year at Christmas (and it seems new every year!), the level in which Jesus speaks to us in the Gospels, and, finally, that of the Second Coming at the end of time, bringing with him the ultimate fulfillment of the prophecy.

Right now we are concerned with our personal and parish (or community) preparation for the celebration of Christ's birth at Christmas. We express our need in the Opening Prayer:

Almighty God,
help us to look forward
to the glory of the birth of Christ our Savior . . . .

There is an intimate connection between "the glory of God to be revealed" in prophecy and the "glory of God in the highest." That anthem the angels sing out when Jesus is born, a song which we will make our own in just a few weeks.

If we would sing out with the joyous vigor that that song deserves, if we would truly profit by our celebration of the birth of Jesus into our lives, we need to prepare the way of the Lord and make straight in the wasteland of our personal and communal lives a "highway for our God." We need to get busy on those roadblocks and potholes!

* * *

"See, the Lord is coming and with him all his saints. Then there will be an endless day *(Entrance Antiphon)*.

"In the desert prepare the way of the Lord!" *(Reading I)*.

184   WEDNESDAY OF THE SECOND WEEK OF ADVENT

READING I   Isa 40:25-31
GOSPEL   Matt 11:28-30

Reading I: God describes himself as all-mighty, all-knowing, all-holy; yet he cares for his children; those who hope in him will not grow weary or faint.

Gospel: Jesus invites all to come to him, take up his yoke, learn from him, for he is gentle and humble of heart.

When you think of it, the odds are high against Advent, against turning it into a time of spiritual renewal, a time of conversion. For most people this time of the year's greatest activity, of shopping, correspondence, parties, and a lot of revelry seems hard to Christianize.

Nevertheless, our spiritual needs—the awareness of our sinfulness and loss of true Christian values, the pain, worry, and anguish that are so much a part of life itself, even the fatigue that overwhelms us at day's end—will not be denied. The Church seems to recognize these human needs of ours in today's liturgy. It would be hard to find a prayer more appropriate to our needs than today's Opening Prayer:

> All-powerful Father,
> we wait the healing power of Christ your Son.
> Let us not be discouraged by our weaknesses
> as we prepare for his coming.
> Keep us steadfast in your love.

We receive the divine promise that our prayer will be favorably heard in our two readings today, and we also get considerable help from the Responsorial Psalm:

He gives strength to the fainting;
for the weak he makes vigor abound (Reading I).

He pardons all your iniquities,
he heals all your ills (Responsorial Psalm).

But it is, above all, Jesus in the Gospel whom we need now in this everyday life of ours: "Come to me, all you who are weary who find life burdensome, and I will refresh you." Think of what we have been doing so far this Advent: we have been asking him to come to us, preparing for his birth as best we can in the context of our busy, often painful life; and now he asks us *to come to him*. In a word, he again places the responsibility on us: "Come to me . . . ." Make at least that much effort. Aware of all your needs, come to me. What I have written elsewhere may be of help in grasping his mind: "What kind of rest, Lord Jesus? Surely, it is not a total removal of the burden; there is no tranquilizer involved; it is rather a new meaning that you provide for the burden: our burden becomes yours and yours ours" (*A New Meditating the Gospels*. Collegeville, Minn.: The Liturgical Press, 1977, 213).

Again, how appropriate that Opening Prayer: "Keep us steadfast in your love." Even our love can grow cold and lack strength and warmth. In the end it might well be that the greatest need of our life is for that steadfast love; for it is the only kind of love that can turn this daily anguish into personal and communal conversion. ". . . we await the healing power of Christ your Son." Conversion is healing. Come, Lord Jesus!

Reading I provides us another way to think of the coming Christmas and its meaning. God is he who is supreme, all-powerful, all-knowing, all-holy, all-wise. He is the Creator and Lord of all things and all creatures, including us, of course. Isaiah puts these words in his mouth:

To whom can you liken me as an equal?
says the Holy One.
Lift up your eyes on high
and see who has created these:
He leads out their army and numbers them,
calling them all by name.

It's all so beautiful! As the lovely old song put it: "He's got the whole world in his hands."

But he's got us in his hand, too. This great, infinite Lord is not so distant and almighty that he is unconcerned about us and all our problems. On the contrary:

> Though young men faint and grow weary,
>   and youths stagger and fall,
> They that hope in the Lord will renew their strength,
>   they will soar as with eagles' wings;
> They will run and not grow weary,
>   walk and not grow faint (Reading I).

Not only does our Great God give us this assurance, but he sends his Son to become one of us, one with us in all our human misery; and it is his birthday we will celebrate and that we so look forward to at Christmas.

> The Lord is coming to save his people;
> happy are those prepared to meet him (Gospel Verse).

Come, Lord Jesus, come!

* * *

"Bless the Lord, O my soul; and all my being bless his holy name" *(Responsorial Psalm)*.

"Your souls will find rest, for my yoke is easy and my burden light" *(Gospel)*.

"The Lord our God comes in strength and will fill his servants with joy" *(Communion Verse)*.

185 THURSDAY OF THE SECOND WEEK OF ADVENT

READING I   Isa 41:13-20
GOSPEL   Matt 11:11-15

Reading I: God, calling himself "the Holy One of Israel," reassures his people in their distress, promising his loving care and spelling out the glories of their ultimate triumph.

Gospel: Jesus introduces John the Baptizer to us today, calling him the greatest man born of woman and telling us to "Heed carefully what you hear!"

In meditating on these Advent Masses, we have to keep reminding ourselves that we are not dealing with the distant past—the time before the coming of Christ. Advent is for *now*. We do indeed make our own the divine instruction that God once gave to his people in olden times; we readily take to ourselves the anguished prayers and longing for relief of those suffering people; and we hear and reflect on Jesus' words; but all this is now ours. Advent is for NOW. We too need deliverance, we need conversion, we need assurance that God does indeed care for and love us. And all this is ours in this and every Advent Mass.

What greater assurance can we have, for example, than the Lord's word to us in Reading I:

> I am the Lord your God,
>   who grasp your right hand;
> It is I who say to you, "Fear not,
>   I will help you."

The language and imagery may be ancient and strange to us, for example:

> Fear not, O worm Jacob,
>   O maggot Israel . . . .

But the message is clear: I love you, I care for you.

> I will help you, says the Lord;
>   your redeemer is the Holy One of Israel.

With that kind of assurance, our response cannot but be enthusiastic:

> The Lord is kind and merciful;
>   slow to anger, and rich in compassion.
> I will extol you, O my God and King,
>   and I will bless your name forever and ever.

And the last verse of this Responsorial Psalm provides backing for our conviction that Advent is timeless:

> Your kingdom is a kingdom for all ages,
>   and your dominion endures through all generations.

Advent is for now, it is timeless, because every age will have its generations that will need solemn reminders of the fact that God's lordship is everlasting and that realizing this fact is crucial for their lives. Every generation—ours included—needs that greatest man born of woman, John the Baptizer (see Luke 7:28), to remind them that the "Lord who is kind and merciful; slow to anger and rich in compassion," is also "the Holy One of Israel," the Creator of all that is, the be-all and end-all of our lives.

Jesus introduces John to us today and from now on John will be confronting us with our sins, our shortcomings, above all, our refusal to recognize God as the Lord of our lives. Ours is the same sin as that of our first parents. John, the preacher of penance, of conversion, belongs with, he is essential to, Jesus the reconciler, the Redeemer. That fact is as true now as it was historically. No Jesus without John. Advent is as simple as that. The Christian life is as simple as that.

So the conversion John will be preaching to us involves more than a change in our ethics, our morality. It is essentially a change of heart, of vision, of insight into the rightful place of God in our lives, an admission deep within that our God is supreme over all life, he is the Holy One of Israel.

"Lord, you are near . . . ." our Entrance Antiphon declares. He is near in so many ways—he sustains the whole world in existence. But today's "Lord, you are near . . . ." may well refer to *the nearness of the conversion that will result in us* when we really realize how essential John's message is for us.

* * *

"The Lord is kind and merciful;
slow to anger, and rich in compassion" *(Responsorial Psalm)*.

"History has not known a man born of woman greater than John the Baptizer. . . . Heed carefully what you hear!" *(Gospel)*.

186 FRIDAY OF THE SECOND WEEK OF ADVENT

READING I   Isa 48:17-19
GOSPEL   Matt 11:16-19

Reading I: The Lord gives his people a program for living, which, if they seek to fulfill it, will bring them great prosperity.

Gospel: Jesus complains about the fickleness of his enemies: neither he nor John the Baptizer can satisfy a "breed" who insist on having a Savior who will satisfy their own perverse ways.

It is obvious to any person who carefully reflects on these Advent readings, psalms, and prayers that the "comings" of God are many and varied. We think especially of the coming of Jesus the Messiah to his people and of the making-present of that historical coming at Christmas; we become aware of a deeper coming of Jesus into our lives if we allow John's words to make straight the way for Christ into our hearts in our prayer, our sacramental experiences, and our reading of Sacred Scripture; and finally we peer into the unknown, far-distant future to Jesus' Second Coming at the end of time.

It should not be too difficult for us to identify the comings of Jesus referred to in today's texts: "The Lord is coming from heaven in splendor to visit his people, and bring them peace and eternal life" (Entrance Antiphon). Christmas will come and go and the world will go on, probably as threatened by war as it is now; so perhaps we ought to look beyond this proximate coming to the one when he will come upon the clouds of heaven in great power and glory.

But our Opening Prayer may well satisfy a more proximate desire:

> All-powerful God,
> help us to look forward in hope
> to the coming of our Savior.
> May we live as he has taught,
> ready to welcome him with burning love and faith.

"Burning love and faith." How do you like that! What a wonderful condition to pray for! This prayer places emphasis on the personal responsibility that all of Christ's comings place upon us. That final peace promised in the Entrance Antiphon will not come without serious preparation for it on the part of all Christians. So, "May we live as he [Jesus] has taught . . . ." (Opening Prayer) by his word and his very being during his first coming among peoples so many years ago!

Then and only then will we be ready to welcome him with burning love and faith in any of his future comings, including his comings to us in the sacraments and that all-important coming of his to us at the moment of our death.

Advent is also a time of hope. Hope, in fact, is perhaps Advent's chief characteristic. Without hope a person (any person) is lost. Our world and each one of us has to live on hope, even as did the people awaiting the Messiah so long ago. Without hope we are all the prey of death. Hope essentially is confidence in the future, looking forward to better times, to fulfillment. A farmer plants his fields and a gardener his or her garden in hope.

I'd like to repeat what I have written elsewhere about another kind of hope: "We talk about our hope in God. Do you know something? The greatest hope, perhaps the only real hope, is God's hope in us. Maybe it's time we start giving him grounds for his hope" (*Loose-Leaf Lectionary,* Collegeville, Minn.: The Liturgical Press, 1981, 2044). God never gives up on us. He never loses hope in us. He never ceases to wait for us to open our hearts and lives to him and to his saving word.

The only way we can grant God that favor is by listening to Jesus and opening up to him a straight way into our inner convictions, our hearts. We surely cannot grant him that favor if we insist on having our personal choice in the kind of Savior we want or in the way we would like to follow that Savior. We have to accept God's idea of a Messiah and his idea is none other than our Lord Jesus Christ. He and he alone will be able to "transfigure our lowly bodies into copies of his own glorious body" (Communion Antiphon).

* * *

"Those who follow you, Lord, will have the light of life" *(Responsorial Psalm).*

"The Lord will come; go out to meet him!
He is the prince of peace" *(Gospel Verse).*

"May we live as he has taught,
ready to welcome him with burning love and faith" *(Opening Prayer).*

187 SATURDAY OF THE SECOND WEEK OF ADVENT

READING I   Sir 48:1-4; 9-11
GOSPEL   Matt 17:10-13

Reading I: Long after he lived, Elijah's life is reviewed by the author of Sirach: he preached penance, was taken to heaven, was a reconciler.

Gospel: Jesus, speaking of the tradition that Elijah is to come again, says that he has already come in the person of John the Baptizer and was rejected.

The prophet Elijah is one of the most important figures of the Old Testament. His name means "Yahweh is my God." His life indicated how he sought fearlessly to try to make Yahweh not only his God but the only God of all his people. He did his work well, and Reading I reviews some of it for us. But even after having been taken to heaven at his death, he lived on in legend and expectation in the lives of his people.

When Jesus and his three favored disciples, Peter, James, and John, were coming down the mountain after his transfiguration, the disciples recall that Moses and Elijah were speaking to Jesus transfigured before them, so they ask him about one of those legendary expectations: "Why do the scribes claim that Elijah must come first [i.e., before the Messiah]?" Jesus' answer is mysterious: Elijah *is* coming and he *has already* come. But he was not recognized and "they [some of the scribes and Pharisees] did as they pleased with him." Jesus is obviously identifying Elijah with John the Baptizer whose summons to penance was likewise rejected.

These Advent Masses continue to force us to face up to our human condition. We are already redeemed by Christ's death and resurrection, but we still need redemption. We so need help to *stay* redeemed, to become more and more redeemed so that we may be true to our vocation and be revealed as "children of light" (Opening Prayer), who can show the way to Christ to the countless peoples who have not yet opened their minds and hearts to Christ.

> Come, Lord, from your cherubim throne; let us see your face, and we shall be saved (Entrance Antiphon).
>
> Lord,
> let your glory dawn to take away our darkness (Opening Prayer).

Elijah's name means "Yahweh is my God." Now, during this Advent, I have to ask myself, "Is Yahweh my God, too? Do I live for him, do I live on him, do I seek to share him with others, as Elijah did?" If my answer to these questions is no, then I need Advent; above all, I need John the Baptizer and his message of repentance:

> Prepare the way for the Lord, make straight his paths:
> all mankind shall see the salvation of God (Gospel Verse).

Christmas is coming. We will have a making-present-again, an "instant replay," as it were, of his birth into our lives, our hearts, but only on condition that we want him badly enough to at least try to rid ourselves of our malice. "I am coming quickly, says the Lord, and will repay each man according to his deeds" (Communion Antiphon). For some who need it, that may be a threat. If our deeds have been evil, the payment will be accordingly. But may we not also take this promise as a divine message of hope and consolation?

53

If, out of the fullness of our human condition, with all its anguish and agony, our consciousness of our sinfulness, we cry: "Come, Lord, do not delay, he will repay us according to our deeds," that is, according to our longing desire for him.

> Lord, make us turn to you,
> let us see your face and we shall be saved.
> O shepherd of Israel, hearken . . . .
> Rouse your power,
> and come to save us (Responsorial Psalm).

* * *

"Lord,
let your glory dawn to take away our darkness" *(Opening Prayer).*

"Prepare the way for the Lord, make straight his paths. . . ." *(Gospel Verse).*

". . . free us from our sins,
and prepare us for the birthday of our Savior . . . ." *(Prayer After Communion).*

7   THIRD SUNDAY OF ADVENT   Cycle A

READING I   Isa 35:1-6, 10   **READING II**   James 5:7-10
GOSPEL   Matt 11:2-11

Reading I: The prophet describes the joy of all nature when the exiles are allowed to return to their homeland, and he attributes the rescue to the Lord himself.

Reading II: James shares the belief of his fellow apostles that Jesus will return soon; he counsels patience with the Lord and with one another.

Gospel: Jesus reassures John in prison that he is truly the Messiah, for he fulfills all the works foretold of the Messiah by the prophets.

> Lord God,
> may we, your people,
> who look forward to the birthday of Christ
> experience the joy of salvation
> and celebrate that feast with love and thanksgiving (Opening Prayer).

We are in the midst of the Christmas rush, and I think most of us have to admit that it is pretty painful. The persuasiveness of the advertisements on TV, radio, and in magazines and newspapers becomes more intense and disagreeable year by year. The artificiality of it all is liable to make us cynical—and hypocritical. It is easy for us to become overly critical of the way we Americans demean and deform the true meaning of Christmas with all the commercialism attached to it. But we have to be careful lest we lapse into Pharisaism and think to ourselves, "Thank God, I am not like the rest of men . . . ." Who of us does not like to receive gifts? May *we* celebrate the feast with love and thanksgiving.

There is no doubt that people mutilate and caricature the Christmas message. But what right have we to pass judgment on them and their intentions? For all we know, God can make use even of the commercialism and artificiality of the season to penetrate into the minds and hearts of his people, bringing them the true meaning of the feast. He might even succeed in converting a few. As for us who know better, we can listen to St. Paul and "Rejoice in the Lord always; again I say, rejoice! The Lord is near" (Entrance Antiphon).

Besides passing judgment on others (always dangerous to one's spiritual health), there is another danger: that of reacting to the commercialism of Christmas *by over-spiritualizing the feast.* We may never forget that God comes to us where we are—into this material world of the twentieth century and into this particular area of the material world, this particular time of its history. He and his caring come to us in concrete, tangible ways. But is it possible to over-spiritualize Christmas?

In the young Church there was a heresy called Gnosticism that threatened the vitality of early Christianity. Gnosticism hated everything material, especially the human body. According to this philosophy (religion?), anything material or anything connected with the material in man, e.g., sexuality and marriage—anything physical—was hateful and worthy of condemnation. The only thing that mattered was the soul. The Gnostics sought to spiritualize religion to such a degree that religion was effectively cut off from practical living. This heresy was condemned by the Church, but it has probably never been eliminated from the thinking of some of her members.

John the Baptist was hard on himself and he fasted very rigorously. But he was not a Gnostic. He did not welcome physical suffering. In today's Gospel John is in a dungeon, the victim of a petty tyrant and his vengeful, immoral consort. It is just possible that, in the dark, vile hole of a prison John is having some doubts about Jesus as the Messiah; so he sends messengers to Jesus to inquire: "Are you 'He who is to come' or do we look for another?" Jesus' answer clarifies the kind of Messiah John should be looking for. He is not a fulfiller of political dreams, a military leader. He is a Savior, a healer of the whole human person, soul and body.

In Reading I Isaiah describes the coming Messiah as one who will open the eyes of the blind, clear the ears of the deaf, heal the lame and the mute. John knew this and Jesus had confidence in John's faith in Scripture. So he simply tells the messengers: "Go back and report to John what you hear and see: the blind recover their sight, cripples walk, lepers are cured, the deaf hear, dead men are raised to life, and the poor have the good news preached to them." And then comes what may have been a slight but tender rebuke: "Blest is the man who finds no stumbling block in me." We can be sure that John found joy in that reassurance even in his dungeon.

In these real, down-to-earth, concrete, tangible signs, the true Messiah was to be recognized then, and that is the way he is to be recognized in any age, including our own. He came and he comes again this Christmas to teach us to heal, to reconcile, to harmonize, to love—not to dominate, to divide, to overcome. He came to teach us to forgive, to forgive even the Herods and Herodiases of our lives, to forgive unconditionally. Happy are we if we do not lose that faith in Jesus and his messiahship! Happy and blessed are we if we are willing to accept the Messiah on God's terms, not on the terms of any kind of modern over-spiritualization.

The works of mercy, the care of sick minds *and bodies,* still remain the sign whereby the Messiah, his Church, and genuine followers of Jesus are recognized as authentic. The healing, reconciling, forgiving mind of the Lord Jesus must become our mind. If it is, then Christmas will be for us a genuine rebirth, a true renewal, a vivid religious experience. And then we will be able to fulfill the command of Paul in today's Entrance Antiphon: "Rejoice in the Lord always; again I say, rejoice!" Then, too, our Opening Prayer will be answered, and we who look forward to the birthday of Christ will experience the joy of salvation and celebrate that feast with love and thanksgiving.

* * *

"Prepare our hearts and remove the sadness
that hinders us from feeling the joy and hope
which his presence will bestow" *(Alternative Opening Prayer).*

"The Spirit of the Lord is upon me;
he sent me to bring Good News to the poor" *(Gospel Verse)*.

"Say to the anxious: be strong and fear not, our God will come to save us" *(Communion Antiphon)*.

8   THIRD SUNDAY OF ADVENT   Cycle B

READING I   Isa 61:1-2, 10-11   READING II   1 Thess 5:16-24
GOSPEL   John 1:6-8, 19-28

Reading I: The prophet's description of himself as one who brings glad tidings to the captives and one who rejoices in the Lord are to be fulfilled in Jesus and his mother, Mary.

Reading II: Paul tells the Thessalonians that they must never cease rejoicing and rendering constant thanks to the Lord for all that he has done for them.

Gospel: The Evangelist John describes John the Baptist as one who claims, not to be Elijah, nor the prophet, but "a voice in the desert, crying out: 'Make straight the way of the Lord.'"

Today we celebrate Gaudete Sunday, the Sunday of Joy in the midst of the Advent penitential season. The opening words of the Mass command us: "Rejoice in the Lord always; again I say, rejoice!" Then St. Paul tells us to rejoice because "the Lord is near." Paul mistakenly thought that Jesus would return in his own lifetime. But Jesus disappointed him. We rejoice because the Lord is near to us in the coming celebration of his birth, made present for us now.

Rejoicing is essential to our Judeo-Christian heritage. Thus Isaiah in today's Reading I:

> I rejoice heartily in the Lord,
>> in my God is the joy of my soul;
> For he has clothed me with a robe of salvation . . . .

Mary, at the beginning of our Christian era, echoes Isaiah's rejoicing and goes beyond it:

> My soul rejoices in my God.
> My being proclaims the greatness of the Lord,
>> my spirit finds joy in God my savior . . . .

God who is mighty has done great things for me,
holy is his name . . . . (Responsorial Psalm).

The Apostle Paul carries on the tradition of rejoicing, not only in his Letter to the Philippians but again today in his comforting message to the Thessalonians: "Rejoice always, never cease praying, render constant thanks; such is God's will for you in Christ Jesus" (Reading II).

Perhaps the chief reaction of many modern Christians to all these recommendations is: "Rejoice? Why rejoice when the world is going to ruin around us, becoming more and more pagan? How do *I* rejoice in the midst of all my problems: inflation, no job, sickness in the family, worry about the children and other dear ones? Rejoice? Tell me more." Surely, God knows all this. Yet today he insists on repeating to all of us that we cannot live either as persons and, above all, as Christians without joy.

But what is joy? Perhaps it is best to begin with what it is not. It is not mere pleasure (although one can certainly rejoice in sights, sounds, readings that reach our hearts through our senses and cause us to praise the Creator of all). Again, joy is not mere satisfaction in possessions (some of the most joyless persons in the world are those who have everything). One of the main causes of joylessness is a tired lack of involvement in the lives, concerns, sufferings of our fellow human beings, and close to this lack of involvement is a refusal to use and develop the talents God has given to us.

The positive elements of joy? It has many ingredients, but certainly the chief one has to be an awareness of our being possessed by God and our possessing him. Mary said: "My soul rejoices in my God. . . . my spirit finds joy in God my savior . . . ." This is coupled with a strong faith in our having been chosen personally by our God to be his own. "In my God is the joy of my soul," says Isaiah, "for he has clothed me with a robe of salvation."

Joy has also been described as a condition of heart and mind which comes from going, reaching out to our neighbor, opening our hearts to them, becoming involved in their sufferings as well as their joys. It is hard to imagine any person expecting joy in his/her life without this basic Christ-like concern for all who are troubled in any way. We experience joy in the measure that we give and share it.

Perhaps the greatest source of joy is the experience of forgiveness—the experience of forgiving and being forgiven. That is why the greatest joy is possessed by God, whose essential nature and work is forgiveness. We recall Jesus' words: "I tell you, there will likewise be more joy in heaven over one repentant sinner than over ninety-nine righteous people who have no need to repent" (Luke 15:7). We can all experience something of God's joy in forgiving when we forgive one another—not just once, but again and again (the way he does with us). There is one joy we can have that is impossible for God: the joy of *being* forgiven . . . by him and by those we have offended.

A great source of true joy comes from entering enthusiastically into the spirit, the mood, the meaning of the words, songs, and contents of liturgical celebrations like the coming feasts of Christmas and Epiphany. The joy of Mary, Joseph, the shepherds and angels that first Christmas can be ours for the asking in just a few days. "Rejoice . . . . the Lord is near." This is not pretending. It is reality that we celebrate; and so we pray:

Father . . .
the earth rejoices in hope of the Savior's coming . . . .
Prepare our hearts and remove the sadness
that hinders us from feeling the joy and hope
which his presence will bestow . . . . (Alternative Opening Prayer).

* * *

"I rejoice heartily in the Lord,
in my God is the joy of my soul . . . ." *(Reading I)*.

"There is one among you whom you do not recognize—the one who is to come after me—the strap of whose sandal I am not worthy to unfasten" *(Gospel)*.

"Say to the anxious: be strong and fear not, our God will come to save us" *(Communion Antiphon)*.

9   THIRD SUNDAY OF ADVENT   Cycle C

READING I   Zeph 3:14-18   READING II   Phil 4:4-7
GOSPEL   Luke 3:10-18

Reading I: The prophet tells the people of Jerusalem to rejoice and fear not because the Lord is in their midst and has removed judgment from them.

Reading II: Paul tells the Philippians to rejoice in the Lord always, and he connects joy with peace, "which is beyond all understanding."

Gospel: Touched by John's call to repentance, the people ask him, "What ought we to do?" And he tells them.

For the Third Sunday Masses of each of the Cycles A, B, and C, the prayers, the entrance and Communion antiphons are the same, but the readings are from different sources. Yet even in them there is much the same message: they all summon us to cultivate a spirit of joy in our lives, and in each John continues to preach conversion.

Today Zephaniah tells us:

> Shout for joy . . . !
>   sing joyfully . . . !
> Be glad and exult with all your heart . . . .
> The Lord has removed the judgment against you . . . .
> The Lord, your God, is in your midst,
>   a mighty savior . . . .

He goes on to say that God himself will rejoice over us with gladness and renew us in his love:

> He will sing joyfully because of you,
>   as one sings at festivals.

The same sentiments are expressed even more beautifully by Isaiah in the Responsorial Psalm:

> Cry out with joy and gladness:
>   for among you is the great and Holy One of Israel.
>> God indeed is my savior;
>>   I am confident and unafraid.
>> My strength and my courage is the Lord,
>>   and he has been my savior. . . .
>> Give thanks to the Lord, acclaim his name . . . .
>> Sing praise to the Lord for his glorious achievement . . . .
>>   for great in your midst
>>   is the Holy One of Israel!

St. Paul's Letter to the Philippians enlarges on the entrance antiphons we have tried to follow in all the Third Sunday Masses: "Rejoice in the Lord always! I say it again. Rejoice! . . . The Lord himself is near. Dismiss all anxiety from your minds . . . . Then God's own peace, which is beyond all understanding, will stand guard over your hearts and minds, in Christ Jesus."

So there can be no doubt about God's will, his desire, even his command. He knows, as we do not, how essential rejoicing is to our faith, our peace of mind. We could question if it would be possible to be a Christian without joy. And the reason is clear: the Lord is near, the Lord is in our midst. Zephaniah anticipates Jesus' own teaching: "Where two or three are gathered together in my name, there am I in the midst of them . . . . I am with you always . . . ." He is Emmanuel—God-with-us.

Jesus (and Zephaniah) are talking about the Church, the People of God, the Body of Christ. He is talking about every gathering of Christians anywhere, but, above all, at holy Mass. The Spirit of Jesus is the living bond, uniting us all into one, even as members of a human body are united into one by reason of a single life-principle. And because he, the Lord Jesus, is in our midst, our call, our vocation, is to rejoice.

The question is: have we discovered that presence yet? Do we really believe it? To answer these questions, we have to ask ourselves, "How much joy is there in our lives?" If there is little or none, what is the cause? Is it lack of faith in God's own word? One of the paradoxes of history is that Christians, whose hallmark is supposed to be joy, have succumbed in large numbers to heresies like Manicheism, Jansenism, and Puritanism, which allow no joy whatsoever. Too many who call themselves Christians do not only allow, they cultivate gloom and sadness as a constant mentality.

The lack of joy in our liturgical celebrations—even such glorious ones as Christmas and Easter—is one of the great problems of evangelization today: how can we expect to attract non-Christians to our Catholic faith or how can we expect to *keep* our young people if there is no joy, no real rejoicing, evident in our faces, our lives, above all, in our liturgical celebrations?

But what is joy? Attempts to answer that question are made in the other meditations for this Sunday (Cycles A and B). Joy is difficult to define. It is easier to say what it is *not*. It is not self-pity. It is not pessimism, certainly not anxiety. It is not to be found in those who are overly critical of others, and especially not in those who have a low opinion of themselves. The dictionary defines joy very inadequately as "A very glad feeling, great pleasure, delight; happiness." But joy is more than a party which artificially creates "joy."

My personal view is that joy arises primarily out of a sense of our being loved, cherished, esteemed, accepted for who and what we are. The early Christians were the most joyous of people because they saw their baptism as the certain sign and proof that God had loved and chosen them to be his own. Joy is related to hope, expectation, longing—which is why we pray after the Lord's Prayer at Mass:

> . . . protect us from all anxiety
> as we wait in joyful hope
> for the coming of our Savior, Jesus Christ.

Joy is the refusal to give in to pessimism, dismay, gloom or despair; a refusal, above all, to give in to any kind of defeatism. During this holy season of Advent, we have been praying and longing for the coming of the Savior: "Come, Lord, do not delay. . . . Drop down dew, ye heavens, from above." Today Paul tells us that the Lord is near. As already mentioned, we know that Paul was definitely thinking of the Second Coming of Christ at the end of time.

We know, of course, that the Lord is near because Christmas, the making-present-again of his birth, is near. But perhaps we could even claim a different way in which the Lord is near for us: it is in the sense that *we are nearer to him,* that, as a result of our careful preparation (maybe even as a result of these daily meditations), we are closer to believing really and at long last that he is truly *in our midst now,* and therefore we can rejoice and he can exult with joy over us, that he will renew us in his love and dance with shouts of joy over us.

> Father of our Lord Jesus Christ . . . .
> Prepare our hearts and remove the sadness
> that hinders us from feeling the joy and hope
> which his presence will bestow . . . . (Alternative Opening Prayer).

* * *

"The King of Israel, the Lord, is in your midst,
you have no further misfortune to fear" *(Reading I).*

"Present your needs to God in every form of prayer and in petitions full of gratitude" *(Reading II).*

"Say to the anxious: be strong and fear not, our God will come to save us" *(Communion Antiphon).*

188 MONDAY OF THE THIRD WEEK OF ADVENT

READING I   Num 24:2-7, 15-17
GOSPEL   Matt 21:23-27

Reading I: Balaam foresees a happy future for Israel, especially with the
arising of a star from Jacob and a staff from Israel.

Gospel: Jesus gets tired of being constantly picked on by his enemies
and refuses to tell them by whose authority he acts.

NOTE: *If today is December 17 or 18, omit this Mass and use the one
given for the weekdays of Advent, numbers 194 or 195.*

I've often mentioned—and repeat here again—that Advent is not intended to take us on a trip via our imagination back into the pre-
Christian era when the Jews were looking forward with such longing for the coming of a Messiah. We live now. The Savior promised
by the Old Testament prophets has come and has done his saving
work for humankind; he has reconciled humankind with the
Father. Jesus was a divine messenger, the very Son of God himself,
who shared this human life of ours, who experienced all the pain,
hard work, worry, disappointments, and agony of any normal family, any normal person.

So what are we doing with all these pre-Christian prophecies
that describe and foretell a Savior? We use them to clothe *our*
needs, desires and hopes, above all, our heartfelt prayers for help,
light, and guidance in this life of ours, whether our need be personal, family, Church, or national life. Few if any modern poets or
essayists have ever equaled the depth and poignancy of human
anguish expressed in the inspired psalms. Nor could anyone give
such heartfelt expression to the hope for deliverance, understanding, and guidance that is expressed in the psalms and prophets.

Moreover, we give expression to these hopes and longings in
the context of preparation and expectation of a real event, the
making-present-again of the Savior's birth in this year's liturgical
celebration, along with his birth into our hearts and lives.

So we pray:

> Lord,
> hear our voices raised in prayer.
> Let the light of the coming of your Son
> free us from the darkness of sin.
> (Opening Prayer)

Can anyone doubt our personal need for a favorable answer to such
a prayer? It surely provides us with a different understanding of sin
than we are accustomed to, i.e., sin as primarily violation of a com-

mandment. It is that, but more basically sin is a repudiation, great or small, of the love-relationship that God desires with us—it is a rejection of his love and when it becomes habitual, it can easily blind us to all goodness and beauty. So today's prayer is really a wonderful "Act of Contrition":

> Let the light of the coming of your Son
> free us from the darkness of sin.

But true contrition is more than recognizing one's need for forgiveness; such awareness is always easy to come by (at least, for most people). What we all need most of all is "a firm purpose of amendment," leading to lasting conversion. It would be hard to improve on the "firm purpose" which the Communion Antiphon provides today: "Come to us, Lord, and bring us peace. We will rejoice in your presence and serve you with all our heart." It may well be that the trouble with most of our purposes of amendment in the past was that they were not sufficiently permeated with rejoicing at Christ's presence in our midst.

The Gospel provides us with a picture of how *not* to rejoice in Christ's presence. Some of his enemies among the Temple priests want him to provide them with credentials for his teaching and miracles. Before we ridicule too loudly the silliness of their request, it might be good for us to examine the silly excuses we often concoct for refusing Jesus entrance into our love-life and practice.

It's much more comfortable for us to return to the expression of further needs in our lives contained in this Mass, particularly our need to live without fear and our need to pray for guidance. Fear is one of the deadliest enemies of a true relationship with Christ. He often had to ask his disciples, "Why are you fearful, O you of little faith?" The implication was: he was with them, so why should they fear anything? But fear is so common because all of us are so terribly vulnerable.

What we fear most is misfortune for our loved ones. So we need the assurance contained in today's Entrance Antiphon: "Our Savior is coming. Have no more fear."

* * *

"A star shall advance from Jacob,
   and a staff shall rise from Israel" *(Reading I).*

"Your ways, O Lord, make known to me;
   teach me your paths,
Guide me in your truth and teach me,
   for you are God my savior" *(Responsorial Psalm).*

64

189 TUESDAY OF THE THIRD WEEK OF ADVENT

READING I   Zeph 3:1-2, 9-13
GOSPEL   Matt 21:28-32

Reading I: The prophet voices God's dismay at the conduct of his people and predicts a coming age in which loyalty to him and his will will reign supreme.

  Gospel: Jesus contrasts two sons: one who says he will obey his father and refuses, the other who at first refuses obedience but then relents and obeys. His favorite is obviously the latter, the sinner who repents.

   NOTE: *If today is December 17 or 18, omit this Mass and use the one given for the weekdays of Advent, numbers 194 or 195.*

Sin is a fact of life, a fact of human history. People often ask, ''Why did God create people capable of sin?'' A useless question. Who are we to ask God why he did what he wanted to do? Why not settle for the fact that he gave humans the gift of free will. Surely, it was a risk, but one he thought worth taking, precisely because if people had no freedom, they would be incapable of loving, incapable of allowing themselves to be loved, incapable of repentance; for only a free person can decide to return to God, as did the tax collectors and prostitutes Jesus praises in today's Gospel.

    Since we are human and free, we are all more or less acquainted with sin. There are many ways of defining sin, the commonest one being that sin is disobedience of one of God's commandments. But more basically, it is rejecting God's will for us, turning back his love. It is a refusal to give him complete control over our lives, and this results in alienation or estrangement from God. We are the ones who do the estranging, not he.

    Sin does not harm God. It harms us, and often in strange, mysterious ways. One of the most distressing effects of sin is that it makes some of us think we are so damaged by past sins that even God cannot or will not forgive us. ''I'm no good,'' they think. Such thinking is against the entire content and context of Sacred Scripture. Jesus died in order to reconcile all humankind, *all* sinners, with God. In his eyes no sin, great or small, can possibly turn anyone into a ''no-good'' person, unworthy of the Lord's merciful forgiveness. We *have to* believe that.

    Advent is a time for conversion, repentance, returning to God if one has become alienated from him. Today's Mass is much concerned, not only with our need for repentance but with giving us an understanding of what repentance really is. It involves both God and us, but mostly God, and specifically his eagerness to forgive. "The Lord hears the cry of the poor. . . . The Lord is close to the brokenhearted; and those who are crushed in spirit he saves" (Responsorial Psalm).

"Come, O Lord, do not delay: forgive the sins of your people," we pray in the Gospel Verse. But how are we to understand that prayer? Has he not already forgiven us? Could it be that what we are really asking for is that he help us *accept* his loving forgiveness and make our grateful acceptance a "way of holiness"?

Those words, "a way of holiness" belong to Jesus. In today's Gospel he contrasts the mentality of the holy and pious chief priests and elders with that of the tax collectors and the prostitutes. The chief priests and elders apparently didn't think they had been guilty of any sins, and therefore they did not need the repentance and conversion preached by John the Baptizer. The tax collectors and prostitutes had a clearer knowledge of themselves. They believed John, they accepted his "way of holiness" and were reconciled with God and with themselves (I suspect they probably had a party to celebrate the reconciliation).

These are the ones Jesus proposes as models to us. He is not suggesting that we become great sinners in order the better to repent, but rather that we become more willing to allow him and his forgiving love to change us and set us on our own way of holiness.

All this is implicit in today's Opening Prayer:

> Father of love,
> you made a new creation
> through Jesus Christ your Son.
> May his coming free us from sin
> and renew his life within us . . . .

Hopefully, we'll all want to make our Advent confession soon if we haven't already done so. Hopefully, too, we'll all want to see that great and blessed sacrament as God's own idea for granting us his merciful forgiveness and that our lives from now on will be lived according to Christ's way of holiness. Confession is not a time for sadness and anxiety but for celebrating the mercy of God. So:

> I will bless the Lord at all times;
>   his praise shall be ever in my mouth.
> Let my soul glory in the Lord . . . .
>   Look to him that you may be radiant with joy (Responsorial Psalm).

* * *

"The Lord is just; he will award the crown of justice to all who have longed for his coming" *(Communion Antiphon)*.

"The Lord is close to the brokenhearted;
and those who are crushed in spirit he saves"
(Responsorial Psalm).

190 WEDNESDAY OF THE THIRD WEEK OF ADVENT

READING I   Isa 45:6-8, 18, 21-25
GOSPEL   Luke 7:19-23

Reading I: Preaching to the exiles in Babylon, Isaiah reminds them of the Lordship of the God they had abandoned, but promises eventual salvation.

Gospel: From his prison John the Baptizer sends disciples to inquire of Jesus if he is the promised Messiah, and Jesus reassures him by quoting Isaiah's description of the Messiah.

NOTE: *If today is December 17 or 18, omit this Mass and use the one given for the weekdays of Advent, numbers 194 or 195.*

Once again the various "comings" of the Savior—and, above all, the people's longing for the comings—confront us in today's Mass. The one element they all have in common is that the Savior is conceived by the people as one who is indeed a Savior, a rescuer, a deliverer, no matter what may be the nature of human need.

Isaiah in Reading I both promises and prays for a Savior for his people:

Let justice descend, O heavens, like dew from above,
    like gentle rain let the skies drop it down.
Let the earth open and salvation bud forth . . . .

I wish there were space to comment on the beauty and picturesqueness of that kind of language! Isaiah is preaching to people who are in terrible need—the Jews exiled in Babylon. They had refused to remember their total dependence on God, and their forgetfulness brought on the destruction of the Holy City and its holiest treasure, the Temple of God itself:

I am the Lord, there is no other;
    I form the light, and create the darkness . . . .
    There is no just and saving God but me.

Turn to me and be safe . . . .
In the Lord shall be the vindication and the glory
of all the descendants of Israel.

The Savior promised by Isaiah in today's and other sections of Isaiah's prophecy did come. John the Baptizer, while still in his mother's womb, recognized Jesus' presence in Mary's womb and "leapt for joy" (Luke 1:44). John recognized Jesus again when the latter came to ask for baptism, and he tried to dissuade him, saying: "I should be baptized by you, yet you come to me!" (Matt 3:14). The Evangelist John reports John's words when he sees Jesus passing by: "Look! There is the Lamb of God!" (John 1:36).

Now John sends two of his disciples to ask Jesus: "Are you 'He who is to come' or are we to expect someone else?" (Gospel). What has happened to John? The great theologian Romano Guardini is not afraid to admit that John, crying out from his dungeon torture, actually had experienced a moment of doubt about Jesus and needed to be reassured. After all, John was human and doubt is our human heritage.

Jesus' way of convincing John is simple and effective: he quotes the Isaian prophecy which tells of the works to be done by the promised Messiah: "The blind recover their sight, cripples walk, lepers are cured, the deaf hear, dead men are raised to life, and the poor have the good news preached to them. Blest is that man who finds no stumbling-block in me" (Gospel). In other words, "Don't lose faith, John. Hang in there. You are suffering terribly, you will be martyred, but so will I. This is the price we both must pay for redemption—this is the cost of love. If humankind can see how much we have loved them, they may come to love the Father. And that will be worth the cost."

Is it too impossible to believe that Jesus had us also in mind here? We may not be locked in dark dungeons, but the dungeons of our suffering are relative to the strength and courage of each person. Suffering overwhelms, may cause despair, may very easily cause us to lose faith in Jesus. So the whole point of the Gospel is that we may need reassurance as much as John, maybe even more.

The Opening Prayer today is most timely:

Father, may the coming celebration of the birth of your Son
bring us your saving help . . . .

Each of us knows the nature of the "saving help" we want and need. One thing is certain: if it does not stir up our faith in Jesus, it will be only temporary and will do little to "prepare us for eternal life," and that's what matters in the end.

But the coming celebration of Jesus will hardly achieve its best possible purpose if we do not prepare ourselves well for it each remaining day of Advent by intensifying our longing and hunger for Jesus and his love. The Prayer After Communion gives us further insights into the desired preparation:

> God of mercy,
> may this eucharist bring us your divine help,
> free us from our sins,
> and prepare us for the birthday of our Savior,
> who is Lord for ever and ever.

In the end we always come back to the Eucharist. What would we do without it?

* * *

"Let the clouds rain down the Just One,
and the earth bring forth a savior" *(Responsorial Psalm)*.

"Blest is the man who finds no stumbling-block in me" *(Gospel)*.

"The Lord our God comes in strength and will fill his servants with joy" *(Communion Antiphon)*.

191 THURSDAY OF THE THIRD WEEK OF ADVENT

READING I   Isa 54:1-10
GOSPEL   Luke 7:24-30

Reading I: Speaking through the prophet, the Lord promises deliverance to his people, Israel. He uses the tenderest terms to assure them of his enduring love.

Gospel: Jesus assures his hearers that John is the promised precursor and is the greatest man born of woman.

NOTE: *If today is December 17 or 18, omit this Mass and use the one given for the weekdays of Advent, numbers 194 or 195.*

Today's Gospel follows immediately after Jesus had sent John's disciples back to him with a message of reassurance for John: I am indeed the Messiah for whom you prepared the way by your preaching of repentance and your austere life: trust me. It is now

69

the most natural thing in the world for Jesus to give voice to his own estimation of his great cousin and precursor. "What did you go out to see [in the desert]—a prophet?" he asks the crowd, most of them admirers and converts of John. "He is that . . . and something more. This is the man of whom Scripture says, 'I send my messenger ahead of you to prepare your way before you.'"

Then comes his greatest tribute to John: "I assure you, there is no man born of woman greater than John. Yet the least born into the kingdom of God is greater than he." (They have Jesus and the fullness of his teaching, which John did not have. The entire passage hardly reveals the depth and extent of the love and admiration Jesus had for John.)

The latter part of the Gospel reveals how readily the majority of Jesus' hearers agreed with him. They had accepted John's message of conversion and experienced the joy of reconciliation with God and their own consciences. They had turned their lives around. On the other hand, the Pharisees and lawyers refused to heed John and "they defeated God's plan in their regard." God's plan, his will and desire is that all sinners return to him who alone can give peace of mind and joy. These men resisted—they preferred their own way. They knew better than John. They knew better than God.

Perhaps at this stage of Advent it would be healthy for us to ask ourselves: "To which group do I belong—with the admitted but repentant sinners or with those who reject John's preaching and defeat God's plan in our regard?"

"Lord, you are near, and all your commandments are just; long have I known that you decreed them for ever" (Entrance Antiphon). He is indeed near. Only a few days remain before we celebrate his birth again. Christmas will be just another day for us—it will leave us unchanged and restless unless John can get through to our inner being. So our prayer today is both necessary and instructive:

> Lord,
> our sins bring us unhappiness.
> Hear our prayer for courage and strength.
> May the coming of your Son
> bring us the joy of salvation.

It seems reasonable to imagine the Lord's response to that prayer: the coming of my Son will indeed bring you the joy of salvation *if* you first accept John into your lives and allow him to prepare you. Or perhaps, instead of my trying to put words into God's mouth, it would be more effective to listen to his own thoughts:

The Lord calls you back,
   like a wife forsaken and grieved in spirit . . . .
But with enduring love I take pity on you,
   says the Lord, your redeemer. . . .
Though the mountains leave their place
   and the hills be shaken,
My love shall never leave you . . .
   says the Lord, who has mercy on you (Reading I).

So, while there is still time, may we all:

Prepare the way for the Lord, make straight his paths:
all mankind shall see the salvation of God (Gospel Verse).

It's hard to surpass the description of the ideal Advent life given in today's Communion Antiphon: "Let our lives be honest and holy in this present age, as we wait for the happiness to come when our great God reveals himself in glory."

*   *   *

". . . with enduring love I take pity on you,
   says the Lord, your redeemer" *(Reading I)*.

"I will praise you, Lord,
for you have rescued me" *(Responsorial Psalm)*.

"I send my messenger ahead of you to prepare your way before you" *(Gospel)*.

192 FRIDAY OF THE THIRD WEEK OF ADVENT

READING I   Isa 56:1-3, 6-8
GOSPEL   John 5:33-36

Reading I: Isaiah foretells an era when the house of the Lord will be called a house of prayer for all peoples, not just the Jews.

Gospel: Once again Jesus bears witness to the greatness of John: he was a lamp, lighting the way for the coming of the Messiah.

NOTE: *If today is December 17 or 18, omit this Mass and use the one given for the weekdays of Advent, numbers 194 or 195.*

The theme of the Second Coming of Christ at the end of time seems to predominate in today's Mass: "The Lord is coming from heaven in splendor to visit his people, and bring them peace and eternal life" (Entrance Antiphon). It is only at the Second Coming that the prophecy of Isaiah in Reading I can be fulfilled:

> . . . my house shall be called
> a house of prayer for all peoples. . . .
> Others will I gather to him
> besides those already gathered.

Universal peace—with all peoples reconciled with one another and with their God—is an ideal that the national antagonisms and armed conflicts of our age make more and more appealing. As never before in history, the "end times" foretold by Isaiah and anticipated by early Christians seem more and more possible. Universal peace has never before been more desirable.

St. Paul in Phil 3:20-21 gives us some idea of what the Second Coming will do for each of us personally: "We are waiting for our Savior, the Lord Jesus Christ, he will transfigure our lowly bodies into copies of his own glorious body" (Communion Antiphon). I suspect that that condition of possessing glorified bodies is going to be much more satisfying than we now imagine.

Our immediate preoccupation is our present condition and needs, the needs of our world, too:

> Come, Lord, bring to us your peace;
> let us rejoice before you with a perfect heart (Gospel Verse).

Somehow, by now we are convinced that the coming celebration of Christ's birth is full of potential for making our present lives more gratifying than they have been and are; so we pray:

> All-powerful Father,
> guide us with your love
> as we await the coming of your Son.
> Keep us faithful
> that we may be helped through life
> and brought to salvation.

Through Isaiah, his prophet, the Lord himself provides us with some directives for helping us to help ourselves:

> Observe what is right, do what is just . . . .
> Happy is the man who does this;
> the son of man who holds to it;
> Who keeps the sabbath free from profanation,
> and his hand from any evildoing (Reading I).

Again Jesus presents us with the image of his precursor John, calling him "the lamp, set aflame and burning bright, and for a while you exulted willingly in his light" (Gospel). But he leaves it to us to carry through on that idea, hoping that we will be more successful in heeding John's summons to conversion and repentance than his hearers. He simply goes on to say: "I have testimony greater than John's, namely, the works the Father has given me to accomplish. These very works which I perform testify on my behalf that the Father has sent me."

Here we are, with Christmas only a few days in the future, beset with a variety of ills, spiritual, physical, and mental. "Lord, we are nothing without you" (Prayer Over the Gifts). We have lived through three weeks of Advent, of spiritual renewal with John the Baptist as our retreat master, standing before us, haunting us, calling us to turn our lives around. It is still not too late. With our sisters and brothers all over the world, we pray:

> May God have pity on us and bless us;
> may he let his faith shine upon us. . . .
> May God bless us,
> and may all the ends of the earth fear him! (Responsorial Psalm).

* * *

"The Lord is coming from heaven in splendor to visit his people, and bring them peace and eternal life" *(Entrance Antiphon)*.

"Come, Lord, bring to us your peace;
let us rejoice before you with a perfect heart" *(Gospel Verse)*.

"We are waiting for our Savior, the Lord Jesus Christ; he will transfigure our lowly bodies into copies of his own glorious body" *(Communion Antiphon)*.

For Saturday, see pages 82ff.

READING I   Isa 7:10-14   READING II   Rom 1:1-7
GOSPEL   Matt 1:18-24

Reading I: We hear the ancient prophecy given to King Ahaz that a "virgin shall be with child, and bear a son . . ." whose name shall be "Immanuel."

Reading II: Paul claims to have been called by God to preach the Gospel according to God's Son, "who was descended from David according to the flesh . . . ."

Gospel: Matthew tells us how the Lord informed Joseph of Mary's pregnancy and how Joseph is to name the child "Emmanuel," a name which means "God is with us."

Let the Lord enter; he is king of glory (Responsorial Psalm).

There is a sense of urgency, or more exactly, expectancy, in today's liturgy. It is much deeper and more authentic than the eagerness with which children await Christmas Eve and Santa Claus. One might believe and hope that it rises from our hearts, from the deep needs of our wounded, vulnerable humanity. "Let the clouds rain down the Just One, and the earth bring forth a Savior" (Entrance Antiphon). Our prayer is appropriate:

Lift our minds in watchful hope
to hear the voice which announces his glory
and open our minds to receive the Spirit
who prepares us for his coming.

There is also a sense of urgency and insistence on the part of God. Today's texts indicate how very much he insists on entering our lives. Ahaz tries to resist, but God will not take no for an answer. "The virgin shall be with child, and bear a son, and shall name him Immanuel" (Reading I). To Joseph the Lord's messenger appears in a dream and says: "Have no fear about taking Mary as your wife. It is by the Holy Spirit that she has conceived this child. She is to have a son and you are to name him Jesus because he will save his people from their sins."

So all the initiative is from God: he is filled with an irrepressible desire and determination to *enter our lives,* to *live with us,* to *live in* us, to *save* us. "The Lord himself will give you this sign. . . ."

There is another theme in today's readings, namely, the *names* of the promised Redeemer. The angel tells Joseph that he is to give the child the name JESUS, "because he will save his people from their sins." It has been said that all the rest of the New Testament is a commentary on that statement, enlarging it, applying it to our human existence. We'll come back to the other name shortly.

What is the nature of this salvation that Jesus will bring? Christ's salvation is for the *whole person;* not just for the soul, but soul and body, work, play, business and home, personal life and home life, all ages of the human person. He will save his people from their sins. What does that mean? We usually think of salvation almost exclusively in terms of our souls at the end of our lives —our getting to heaven. This is surely true. But salvation is also for *now.* The promise is that Jesus will save us from our sins right now, in the midst of our everyday life.

> . . . as Christmas draws near
> make us grow in faith and love . . . . (Prayer After Communion).

Salvation at the end of our life is fine, it is essential. But we all need help right now. We need to be saved from specific concrete sins that insure us and others now. Saved from selfishness, from greed, from a bad temper, from envy and jealousy, from hatred, bitterness, resentment, a critical spirit, gossiping—to say nothing of the other weaknesses we give in to. All this Jesus wishes to accomplish in us here and now—if we are willing to be saved in his way. Isn't all this what Jesus did for people in his own lifetime? He gave new life, he healed hearts, forgave sins; above all, he gave *hope,* a new life, a new spirit.

> Father . . . .
> Lift our minds in watchful hope . . . . (Alternative Opening Prayer).

The other name that the Father gives to Jesus is *Immanuel,* which means "God is with us." This means that God *is here,* he is *now,* God is *for us.* St. Paul understood well what Emmanuel meant; he wrote: "If God is for us, who can be against us? . . . he who did not spare his own Son but handed him over for the sake of us all will not grant us all things besides?" (Rom 8:31-32).

These two names JESUS ("God is salvation") and EMMANUEL ("God is with us") contain the whole meaning of Christmas. To be sure, it is not the meaning of Christmas that is generally understood in and by our American way of life, which has done just about everything to destroy that meaning. But God will not be resisted now any more than Ahaz wanted to resist him then. We shall celebrate the birth of Jesus in a few days, and we shall know that God is with us now. God is for us now, lifting us up, trusting in us, hoping in us, never giving up on us. These two names, Jesus and Emmanuel, were in the hearts and on the lips of Mary and Joseph all during the Advent of her pregnancy. We can join them in their prayer in the days remaining till Christmas. Then we will be ready. And we can add the ancient "Maranatha" prayer—"Come, Lord Jesus!"

An afterthought: Perhaps the most appropriate words in all the Bible giving the theme and spirit of this Sunday are those of the Book of Revelation (3:20): "Here I stand, knocking at the door. If anyone hears me calling and opens the door, I will enter his house and have supper with him, and he with me." So . . . . May we all get ready for the knock and unlatch the doors of our hearts. It will be loud and clear. We are certain to hear it. So we pray:

> Lord,
> fill our hearts with your love . . . . (Opening Prayer).

* * *

"Let the clouds rain down the Just One, and the earth bring forth a Savior" *(Entrance Antiphon).*

"The virgin shall be with child
and give birth to a son,
and they shall call him Emmanuel. . . ." *(Gospel).*

11   FOURTH SUNDAY OF ADVENT   Cycle B

READING I   2 Sam 7:1-5, 8-12, 14, 16   **READING II**   Rom 16:25-27
GOSPEL   Luke 1:26-38

Reading I: King David wants to build a temple for God, but God tells him he will do the building: his house and kingdom shall endure forever.

Reading II: St. Paul claims to preach "the gospel which reveals the mystery hidden for many ages but now manifested . . . and . . . made known to all the Gentiles . . . ."

Gospel: Again we hear the familiar, but ever new, account of God's proposal to Mary to be the mother of his Son and Mary's acceptance of the proposal.

One of the most striking aspects of today's liturgy is the contrast between King David and Mary. David wants to *do* something great for God—he wants to build a magnificent temple—and Mary expresses her willingness to *receive* someone great from God, his very own Son: "I am the maidservant of the Lord. Let it be done to me as you say" (Gospel). With that consent her virginal womb became the dwelling place of the Son of God.

Mary's way is the way God wants it—has always wanted it ever since he first created the world and all its creatures: a world, we included, which can always make Mary's word its own:

> God who is mighty has done great things for me,
> holy is his name . . . . (Luke 1:49).

The great Norwegian novelist and convert Sigrid Undset caught this delicate understanding when she wrote:

> When we give each other our Christmas presents in His name, let us remember that He has given us the sun and the moon and the stars, all the earth with its forests and mountains and oceans and all that lives and moves upon them. He gives us all green things and everything that blossoms and bears fruit—all that we quarrel about and all that we have misused. And to save us from our own foolishness and from all our sins, He came down to earth and gave Himself.

All this does not mean that we should not want to do things for God, but simply that we let him do the giving first and *then we respond* with our gifts. The mentality to be avoided is to want to do things for God with the idea of putting him in debt to us, forcing him to do us favors and grant our prayers. Love is an exchange, and unless there is an exchange, a giving, but, above all, a willingness to *receive,* it cannot be genuine. Christmas is *the* great exchange: God gives Jesus and we give our lives, our hearts, for him to dwell in.

"The Lord also reveals to you that he will establish a house for you," the Lord told David through Nathan the prophet. To be sure, he is referring to David's line of descendants, with its greatest figure Jesus the Messiah. But we can also reflect a little on the literal meaning of the word "house." A house, if it is a real home, is a place where one stays, he/she does not just pass through. It is God's will, his determination, to dwell among us, to remain with us, to make himself at home with us. He wants to come into our world, the real world of our lives. But he will come only on condition that we provide hospitality for him, as Mary and Joseph did.

God asked Mary for a home to dwell in for his Son, and she gave her own body. Hers was the best hospitality of all. In her God found human flesh, a body in which he was to dwell and be at home. In her the child took over as new life that changes our life.

We wait for the coming of Christ this week. But he also waits. He waits for our invitation, our "Yes," even as he waited for

Mary's. Henri Nouwen once wrote: "When someone accepts a gift, he admits another into his world and is ready to give him a place in his own being. . . . Ultimately, a gift becomes a gift only when it is accepted" (*With Open Hands,* Notre Dame, Inc.: Ave Maria Press, 1975, 62). This naturally makes us welcome today's Prayer After Communion:

> Lord . . .
> as Christmas draws near
> make us grow in faith and love
> to celebrate the coming of Christ our Savior,
> who is Lord for ever and ever.

We could add: "Make us grow in faith and love *and* the kind of hospitality exemplified by Mary." That's what he is waiting for, our "Yes," our "Do come in and make yourself at home in me and in my life." Are we active receptacles, offering our poor stable, our table, our heart, our flesh to him?

The one way we can be sure of making him welcome is by being open and receptive to one another—to anyone, especially the poor and homeless. Tolstoy once told a story about an old cobbler, Martin, who dreamt that Christ was going to visit him. All day he waited and watched. While he waited he gave hospitality to one person who was cold, to another who needed reconciliation, to another who needed clothing. At the end of the day, he was disappointed that Christ had not come. That night he had another dream, and all those to whom he gave hospitality returned and a voice said, "Martin, do you not know me? I am Jesus. Whatever you do to the least of these you do to me."

It is not only at Christmas that Jesus comes and knocks at the door of our hearts; he comes every day of the year in every brother and sister.

"The Virgin is with child and shall bear a son, and she will call him Emmanuel" (Communion Antiphon). "Your throne shall stand firm forever" (Reading I). The Word is made flesh and dwells among us. This is "the mystery hidden for many ages but now manifested . . . and . . . made known to all the Gentiles that they may believe and obey . . . ." (Reading II). "I am the maidservant of the Lord. Let it be done to me as you say" (Gospel).

"For ever I will sing the goodness of the Lord" (Responsorial Psalm).

* * *

"Let the clouds rain down the Just One, and the earth bring forth a Savior" *(Entrance Antiphon).*

12   **FOURTH SUNDAY OF ADVENT**   **Cycle C**

READING I   **Mic 5:1-4**   **READING II**   **Heb 10:5-10**
GOSPEL   **Luke 1:39-45**

Reading I: Micah foretells that the birthplace of the Messiah is to be Bethlehem and that he will be a shepherd to his people.

Reading II: The author of Hebrews provides us with a theological explanation of the work and motivation of the Messiah.

Gospel: We hear the familiar account of Mary's visit to Elizabeth and the latter's cry of joy: "Blessed are you among women . . . ."

Father . . . .
Lift our minds in watchful hope
to hear the voice which announces his glory
and open our minds to receive the Spirit
who prepares us for his coming (Alternative Opening Prayer).

At this moment those are perhaps our greatest needs—watchful hope and minds opened to receive the Spirit who prepares us for his coming. Those are precisely the gifts that animated Elizabeth, future mother of John, and that allowed her to detect the wonder of the entrance of the Son of God and his mother into her home.

Our readings today are the most significant of Advent.

You, Bethlehem-Ephrathah,
too small to be among the clans of Judah,
From you shall come forth for me
one who is to be ruler in Israel . . . .

Those words are most familiar and dear to us, but they may not be the most meaningful for us. Even more important is the statement of his origin "from of old, from ancient times." The Evangelist John will later be more specific: "In the beginning was the Word . . . ."

And still more important is the statement of the nature of the Messiah's work:

He shall stand firm and shepherd his flock
by the strength of the Lord . . .
And they shall remain, for now his greatness
shall reach to the ends of the earth;
he shall be peace.

Jesus has already fulfilled part of that prophecy, but much of the latter part still remains to be completed. Not all the world knows of his greatness, nor is the world at peace with itself or with its God.

"Lord, make us turn to you, let us see your face and we shall be saved" (Responsorial Psalm). This is the universal cry of all human-kind. It is *the* Advent prayer for us all as we approach the celebration of the Lord's birth. It is intense, fervent:

> O shepherd of Israel, hearken,
> from your throne upon the cherubim, shine forth.
> Rouse your power,
>   and come to save us. . . .
> Then we will no more withdraw from you;
>   give us new life, and we will call upon your name.

Reading II gives us the theology of the work and the motivation of the Messiah. Even before we celebrate his birth, we are reminded of our distant celebration of Good Friday:

> . . . As is written of me in the book,
> I have come to do your will, O God.

These will be Christ's words as he sweats blood in the Garden of Gethsemane, with the result that "By this 'will' we have been sanctified through the offering of the body of Jesus Christ once for all."

There are several things to be noted about this kind of obedience to God's will on the part of Jesus, of Mary, and, hopefully, of us all. First, it is carried out in full freedom; for it is only in freedom that love is possible, and what Jesus and Mary will have in their hearts is the most mature, most perfect kind of love ever made. Second, the obedience was not a kind of stoic resignation to God's will. God's will then and now is a "summons to take responsibility. Jesus and Mary show in their actions a God-given eagerness to be responsible for themselves and for others' good" (Joseph Tetlow, *America,* 141, no. 19 [December 16, 1979] 397), and that includes each one of us.

Mary's kind of obedience is voiced in her consent to become the mother of the Savior:

> I am the servant of the Lord:
> may his will for me be done (Gospel Verse).

Mary's consent to God then hopefully becomes our consent to him now, as we prepare to celebrate Jesus' new birth into our hearts on Christmas Eve and all through the years of our life.

To understand the Gospel we have to recall the background of the angel's announcement to Mary and her acceptance of God's will that she become the Mother of God. Her first reaction to her great Gift and privilege is that of concern for another, her old cousin Elizabeth. She anticipates the attitude that Jesus himself will later demonstrate when he constantly goes out of his way to care for those in any kind of need.

We can be grateful to the Evangelist Luke for his remembrance of the drama related when both Elizabeth and John in her womb understand what is happening here. God comes to them in Mary's womb, and John stirred in his mother's womb. As Caryll Houselander puts it: "John almost danced his way into life" (*The Book of the Savior,* New York: Sheed and Ward, 1952, 13).

As we prepare to celebrate the birth of Jesus, the Messiah-Savior, it may be good for us to reflect on what this celebration should mean for us. If we penetrate through the excitement, the sentimentalism, the commercialism, we may come to grasp that this yearly celebration of the birth of Jesus recalls us to the heart of our faith as Christians and gives us some idea of how we are to react and respond to it. For example, with Elizabeth we can all say: "Who am I that the mother of my Lord should come to me?" We can even go farther and ask ourselves: "Who am I that the Lord himself should come to make himself at home in me, that he should feed me with himself?" The only possible answer to those questions is the old one: "Love does such things."

Most of all, we are reminded of how we are to live as his followers. Jesus comes to us with his mother, both of them wishing to share their attitude of total trust in the Father and all-out obedience to his will. (In the case of Mary, she'd like us to share her faith!) With the grace of this feast, we are going to be able—or at least to try—to say in our hearts: "Here am *I,* Lord, I come to do your will." In that will and only in it is our peace. We must expect everything from Jesus. We will receive in proportion to our expectation and our desire.

* * *

"Lord, make us turn to you. Let us see your face and we shall be saved" *(Responsorial Psalm).*

"Then I said, 'As is written of me in the book,
I have come to do your will, O God'" *(Reading II).*

"I am the servant of the Lord;
may his will for me be done" *(Luke 1:38).*

READING I   Gen 49:2, 8-10
GOSPEL   Matt 1:1-17

Reading I: The patriarch Jacob names his son Judah as the head of his family from whom the Messiah will come.

Gospel: Matthew traces the genealogy of Jesus back to Abraham.

NOTE: *These Masses are to be used between December 17 and 24. If a Sunday occurs during this time, the weekday readings for that day are omitted, but may be used on another day during the week, especially to avoid duplicating the Sunday readings.*

The desire to look for and find one's roots seems to be deeply implanted in human nature. Many of us moderns have a somewhat more difficult time tracing our ancestors than Matthew had with Jesus' forbears. He did it many years after Jesus lived, and if Jesus himself as man was aware of his ancestral line, he must have had to smile a bit. The first ancestor, the father of the family, was Abraham whom we all claim as "our father in faith." He was a noble and good man, but not without some small faults.

The list, after Abraham, contains every variety of human character and disposition. There were saints among them, but also adulterers, prostitutes, and a few crooks. When I first heard this list as a young server, I wondered why it was included in the Gospel, which means "good news." It was only many years later that I could conclude that this list is the best of good news, for it tells us that Jesus is *one of us,* that he is really and truly human, that he belongs to us, that the blood in his veins was human, some of it tainted but it was his. It was this human blood that he was to pour out for us on Calvary.

Being human as we are (but without sin), he knows us and all our troubles and problems, as he also knew the troubles and problems of every one of his ancestors. This kind of knowledge is terribly important for a Savior, as his later public life was to show.

It is his birth as one of us that we are looking forward to with such eagerness. Well, not his birth, because that took place at the appointed time in Bethlehem, as related in Luke's Gospel. What we are looking forward to is our personal *celebration* of that birth, and for us that can be every bit as important and full of meaning as the original one. For we believe that our Eucharistic celebration *makes present again* every moment of Jesus' life, from his birth to his Second Coming at the end of time. "The Desired of all nations is coming, and the house of the Lord will be filled with his glory" (Communion Antiphon).

"The Desired of all nations," the desired of every human heart, including our own:

God our Father,
as you nourish us with the food of life,
give us also your Spirit,
so that we may be radiant with his light
at the coming of Christ your Son,
who is Lord for ever and ever (Communion Prayer).

Note the contrast: the Jesus who is descended from human ancestors is also LORD FOR EVER AND EVER!

He is also divine Wisdom incarnate. So we pray:

Come,
Wisdom of our God most High,
guiding creation with power and love:
teach us to walk in the paths of knowledge (Gospel Verse).

There are paths in all our lives that at times seem so crooked and tortuous and painful to follow—Come, Wisdom Incarnate, comfort us in all our trials: help us to see the light at the end of the tunnel.

Our prayer will be answered: "You heavens, sing for joy, and earth exult! Our Lord is coming; he will take pity on those in distress" (Entrance Antiphon).

Father,
creator and redeemer of mankind,
you decreed, and your Word became man,
born of the Virgin Mary.
May we come to share the divinity of Christ,
who humbled himself to share our human nature . . . .
(Opening Prayer)

So that's what it's all about! That's the incredible blessing our celebration of Christ's birth can give us! God's own Son, Wisdom in Person, is born a human in order to enable us to share in his divinity, his wisdom! "May his name be blessed forever . . . ." (Responsorial Psalm).

* * *

"You heavens, sing for joy, and earth exult! Our Lord is coming; he will take pity on those in distress" *(Entrance Antiphon)*.

"Justice shall flourish in his time,
and fullness of peace forever" *(Responsorial Psalm)*.

READING I   Jer 23:5-8
GOSPEL   Matt 1:18-24

Reading I: Jeremiah prophesies that the Lord "will raise up a righteous shoot to David; as king he shall reign and govern
wisely. . . ."

Gospel: An angel appears to Joseph in a dream and tells him that
Mary's child has been conceived by the power of the Holy
Spirit. He is to be called "Jesus," "Emmanuel," "God is with
us."

God's entrance into the lives of people often causes initial pain and
distress. Today's Gospel tells us nothing about Joseph's agony upon
discovering that his beloved fiancée, Mary, is with child, and he
knows he is not the father. Well, this may be a legitimate instance
when we may use our imaginations and put ourselves in Joseph's
place. He loved Mary very much and had asked her to be his wife.
But her being with child must have seemed like a betrayal. How
could she do this to him? And she says nothing. We can wonder
about that, too. Why didn't she tell him about the angel's promise
to her? The sparseness of the Gospels again becomes evident: they
tell us only what is necessary for us to know and believe.

What is necessary for us to know and believe is that—with or
without pain—God has intervened in the lives of Mary and Joseph.
The world can never again be the same.

It is now time for Joseph's vision. The angel of the Lord appears
to him in a dream and tells him: "Joseph, son of David, have no
fear about taking Mary as your wife. It is by the Holy Spirit that she
has conceived this child. . . ." Such words surely must have
mystified Joseph considerably. But he believes in the dream. He
obeys, takes Mary to his home, and makes her his wife. Again we
can imagine the expectation that must have filled their hearts as
they awaited the birth of this child to whom Joseph will give the
name *Jesus,* which means "Yahweh saves." This child "will save
his people from their sins."

All this happened many centuries ago, but the mystery of it all,
and the love that filled the hearts of Mary and Joseph linger on and
are with us still—mainly because the child born to Mary and named
by Joseph is actually Emmanuel, God-with-us. That's the heart of
the matter. God is with us in and through Jesus, and we look forward with anticipation and joy to our personal and communal celebration of the birthday of this child when, through the mystery and
creative glory of the liturgy, the original birth will be made present

in our midst. "Christ our King is coming, the Lamb whom John pro-claimed" (Entrance Antiphon).

We need preparation so that the coming celebration will find us ready and mean something to us. We need some of the hopeful expectation and longing to see the face of the child that filled the hearts of Mary and Joseph during Mary's pregnancy. And so we pray:

> Lord,
> we receive mercy in your Church.
> Prepare us to celebrate with fitting honor
> the coming feast of our redemption (Prayer After Communion).

Will Christmas make a difference for us this year? How many Christmases have we had in our lives? Do we celebrate and then forget, lapsing back into our old way of thinking and living, as though Christmas had never happened? What good is Christmas if it leaves us unchanged? We undoubtedly need a favorable answer to today's Opening Prayer:

> All-powerful God,
> renew us by the coming feast of your Son
> and free us from our slavery to sin.

Renewal in the depths of our being, freedom from the slavery to sin—these are our true needs. The preaching of John the Baptizer and the coming celebration will help. But what can help more than anything else is to be like Joseph—to believe in his dream and to take Mary and the child she bears into our hearts and lives so that he will be God-with-us, too.

* * *

"Come,
Leader of ancient Israel,
giver of the Law of Moses on Sinai:
rescue us with your mighty power" (Gospel Verse).

"When Joseph awoke he did as the angel of the Lord had directed him and received her into his home as his wife" (Gospel).

"His name will be called Emmanuel, which means God is with us" (Communion Antiphon).

READING I   **Judg 13:2-7, 24-25**
GOSPEL   **Luke 1:5-25**

Reading I: We hear the account of Samson's miraculous conception and of the work the Lord intends him to do for his people.

    Gospel: Luke relates the story of the angel's announcement to Zechariah that his barren wife Elizabeth is to bear a son who will be called John.

Today we have two illustrations from Sacred History showing how God normally works in order to prepare his people for his intervention in their lives. God always prefers to work through people rather than through direct personal intervention. Today's readings tell of the miraculous conception of two such persons, Samson and John the Baptizer. There is much similarity—and a few differences —between the two accounts. First the similarities: both the mothers are barren; it is an angel whom God sends to make the announcement; both men will be abstemious, taking neither wine nor strong drink; both will be consecrated to God; the Spirit of the Lord will be with them; and both will meet violent deaths.

The differences are that in Samson's case the angel makes the divine announcement to his mother, and in John's the announcement is made to the father, Zechariah. Also, the woman believed immediately, whereas Zechariah gave in to doubts about how the promise could possibly be fulfilled, given his wife's barrenness and the old age of both.

We might wonder why the Church chooses these two accounts as part of her preparation for the coming celebration of Jesus' birth. The main reason has to be that the extraordinary conception of both Samson and John tell us clearly that it is God and God alone who saves. Thus we sing in the Responsorial Psalm:

I will treat of the mighty works of the Lord;
   O God, I will tell of your singular justice.

But it is also clear that he does not ordinarily choose to work except in and through men and women. Finally, the Lord obviously is convinced that his comings into the lives of his people *have to be prepared.*

This is still God's way. Samson and especially John are still present to us telling us now that the celebration of Jesus' birth this year will be empty unless we heed their preaching and express a willingness to be converted and "to prepare for the Lord a people well-disposed" (Gospel) for Christ's birth.

There is another consideration: God still wishes to work through humans, and these humans are you and I. He wants to use us, our lives and example, to prepare the way for him into the hearts of the countless numbers of men and women who do not know his Son Jesus, mainly because no one has ever told them about him. But we need the message of John—his cry for repentance and reform of lives—before we will be fit and ready to carry on his and Christ's work. So:

> Lord of mercy . . . .
> Let your power take away our weakness
> and make our offerings holy (Prayer Over the Gifts).

One of the chief purposes of these Advent Masses, especially those close to the feast of Christmas, is to

> Open our hearts in welcome
> to prepare for the coming of our Savior . . . .
> (Prayer After Communion)

and to make us more and more aware of our personal needs as "precursors" of Christ now.

> Father,
> you show the world the splendor of your glory
> in the coming of Christ, born of the Virgin.
> Give to us true faith and love
> to celebrate the mystery of God made man (Opening Prayer).

"Give us true faith and love . . . ." Is there any greater need for us or for our world?

* * *

"Fill me with your praise and I will sing your glory!" *(Responsorial Psalm)*.

"Come,
Flower of Jesse's stem,
sign of God's love for all his people:
save us without delay!" *(Gospel Verse)*

"The dawn from on high shall break upon us, to guide our feet on the road to peace" *(Communion Antiphon)*.

READING I   Isa 7:10-14
GOSPEL   Luke 1:26-38

Reading I: The Lord promises to an unreceptive Ahaz that a "virgin shall be with child . . . and shall name him Immanuel."

Gospel: Luke relates the fulfillment of the prophecy: the Virgin Mary consents to become the mother of the "Son of the Most High."

Great, all-holy, all-powerful, the "king of glory" (Responsorial Psalm)— this is our God, but he is also a "God of love and mercy" (Opening Prayer). This is the God who spoke to Ahaz and tells him to ask for a sign from the Lord, his God. But Ahaz answers: "I will not ask! I will not tempt the Lord!" Hypocrite! So God has to argue with him, practically beg him to accept the promise he wishes to offer. He insists: "Listen . . . . Is it not enough for you to weary men, must you also weary my God? Therefore the Lord himself will give you this sign: the virgin shall be with child, and bear a son, and shall name him Immanuel" (Reading I).

How typical Ahaz is of so many of us! God wants to do great things for us, and we resist. This is often the case with us as individuals, but perhaps it is true of humankind in general. We have an inborn hunger and desire for God, and yet we seem so afraid of assuming the responsibility of receiving him into our lives. How different is Mary, the "virgin" in the promise made to Ahaz, the girl God had chosen to receive his greatest gift, his very own Son. Without hesitation Mary consents: "I am the servant of the Lord. Let it be done to me as you say." Mary launches out into a life of faith and thus becomes the mother of Jesus, but also our mother, the "mother of all the living."

How appropriate our prayer today:

> God of love and mercy,
> help us to follow the example of Mary,
> always ready to do your will.
> At the message of an angel
> she welcomed your eternal Son
> and, filled with the light of your Spirit,
> she became the temple of your Word . . . .

Mary in her life and example is the greatest preacher and spiritual director the world has ever known, that is, apart from the Son she is about to give birth to. The lesson of her life is the only lesson that is essential for us: when God wishes to give himself to us, to do something marvellous for us, we must not refuse, as Ahaz did. Rather, like Mary, we open our minds and hearts and lives to him, and he comes and makes himself at home in us. It's as simple as that. This is basic Christianity.

There is a hollow, empty feeling in all our hearts that only Christ can satisfy. But he cannot come into those hearts and fill them with himself unless we become more hospitable than we are now. Arguing with him makes no sense because he is so terribly persistent. "Listen . . . ! Is it not enough for you to weary men, must you also weary my God?"

To open us up, to soften our resistance to God's blessings, to free us from obstacles to Christ's entrance, in a word, to make us more hospitable, all this is what Advent seeks to do for us. Only if we open our lives to the Lord as Mary did will we become eligible for the promise contained in the Responsorial Psalm:

> He shall receive a blessing from the Lord,
> a reward from God his savior.
> Such is the race that seeks for him,
> that seeks the face of the God of Jacob.

May we who are drawing so close to the making-present-again of Christ's birth in our Christmas celebration cry out with full, fearless hearts: "I am the servant of the Lord. Let it be done to me as you say." Or, to put it another way, "Come, Lord Jesus, come!"

* * *

"A shoot will spring from Jesse's stock, and all mankind will see the saving power of God" *(Entrance Antiphon)*.

"Let the Lord enter; he is king of glory" *(Responsorial Psalm)*.

"Do not fear, Mary. You have found favor with God" *(Gospel)*.

READING I　Song 2:8-14
GOSPEL　　Luke 1:39-45

Reading I:　The author of the Song of Songs describes the love that God has for his people and the longing he has for union with them.

Gospel:　Elizabeth is granted the great privilege of recognizing that Mary is carrying the Savior of the world in her womb.

Love letters and love songs are terribly revealing, but not always too easy to compose—unless the composer is God himself, as is the case with the Song of Songs. This most beautiful of all love songs draws on all kinds of picturesque imagery in order to give some indication of his feelings about his beloved. The imagery in this case is related to the person, the human body. To our puritanical ears it may sound rather daring. But then, of course, our God is daring, besides being the greatest of all lovers. But who is the beloved? It is God's own people, it is us:

> Yes, God so loved the world
> that he gave his only Son,
> that whoever believes in him may not die
> but may have eternal life (John 3:16).

In today's reading the beloved waits in expectation for the coming of the Bridegroom:

> Hark! my lover—here he comes
>   springing across the mountains . . . .
> My lover is like a gazelle . . . .
> My lover speaks; he says to me,
>   "Arise, my beloved, my beautiful one,
>   and come!
> "For see, the winter is past,
>   the rains are over and gone. . . .
> "O my dove in the clefts of the rock . . . .
> Let me see you,
>   let me hear your voice,
> For your voice is sweet,
>   and you are lovely."

We can make those sentiments our own in a very special way today, as we look forward to the coming of our Beloved, the Lord Jesus. He will tell us that the winter of our old life of sin and alienation from him and from one another is past, the time for pruning the vines has come. It is now the hour for our complete personal and community renewal. Whether we realize it or not, this is the way we ought to feel towards our Savior's coming; it is the way he feels towards us, too; for we must not forget that our love for him is a pale image of his love for us. He is the one who longs to possess and be possessed. That's what Reading I tells us.

> Cry out with joy in the Lord, you holy ones;
> sing a new song to him. . . .
> Our soul waits for the Lord . . .
> For in him our hearts rejoice . . . . (Responsorial Psalm).

If anyone has a right to sing the Song of Songs, it is Mary, *the Beloved* of God. She has just said yes to God's wooing of her. She has given herself over to him with utmost abandon, and now she carries his Child, his own divine Son, in her womb.

No sooner does she receive God's Son into her womb than she takes off into the hill country to Zechariah's house where she greets her cousin Elizabeth, who, she feels, needs her in her advanced pregnancy. What kind of greeting is this that makes a child in an old woman's womb leap for joy and almost dance his way into the world! It's not the greeting, it's the one who makes it, the One whom Mary is carrying. How grateful we must be to Elizabeth for having formed for us out of her wonder the prayer to Mary that so beautifully expresses our grateful delight in her and her Son: "Blessed are you among women and blessed is the fruit of your womb!"

We can also wonder with Elizabeth, "Who am I that the mother of my Lord should come to me?" Should come to me, to us, not only at Christmas, but that he comes to us daily in his Word, in the sacrament of his love, the Eucharist.

> Lord. . . .
> May we who celebrate the birth of your Son as man
> rejoice in the gift of eternal life when he comes in glory. . . .
> (Opening Prayer).

* * *

"Soon the Lord God will come, and you will call him Emmanuel, for God is with us" *(Entrance Antiphon)*.

"Come,
Radiant Dawn,
splendor of eternal light, sun of justice:
shine on those lost in the darkness of death!" *(Gospel Verse)*.

"Blessed are you among women and blessed is the fruit of your womb!" *(Gospel)*.

READING I   1 Sam 1:24-28
GOSPEL   Luke 1:46-56

Reading I: Hannah, having conceived a son in answer to prayer, now brings the child to Eli to present him to the Lord.

Gospel: We have the great joy of sharing in the *Magnificat* of Mary.

My heart rejoices in the Lord, my Savior (Responsorial Psalm).

It isn't often in the year's liturgy that the Responsorial Psalm is not a psalm at all but simply a continuation of the Old Testament reading. Such is the case today. But if the Responsorial Psalm has as its main purpose to provide us with a personal response to the Word of God, it would be hard to improve on Hannah's cry of joy and gladness on God's favor to her:

> My heart exults in the Lord,
>   my horn is exalted in my God. . . .
> The bows of the mighty are broken . . . .
> The Lord puts to death and gives life . . . .
> He raises the needy from the dust;
>   from the ash heap he lifts up the poor. . . .

Hannah had begged the Lord for a child, promising that she would offer him back to God if her prayer were answered. The child was born and now she joyfully fulfills her promise: "Now I, in turn, give him to the Lord; as long as he lives, he shall be dedicated to the Lord" (Reading I). She leaves him there and bequeaths to us her prayer of praiseful gratitude.

"My heart rejoices in the Lord, my Savior," and it is obvious why. Because it is God and God alone who does everything for her. This is all the more true of Mary and her prayer of joyous gratitude:

> God who is mighty has done great things for me;
>   holy is his name;
> His mercy is from age to age
>   on those who fear him (Gospel).

In her prayer, but most of all in her person, Mary gathers up all the just ones of her people from their beginning until now. Mary *is* Israel, to put it simply. Not the Israel of alienation from God, but the Israel who lives for the Lord. She cries: "He has upheld Israel his servant, ever mindful of his mercy . . . ." It is no accident that she makes this phrase part of her song of joy.

So we have Hannah and Mary—two Jewish mothers, both blessed by God and both responding to him out of the fullness of their personal experience and tradition. Hannah offers her Son back to God, as Mary will do with Jesus.

But what is all this to and for us besides stirring in us an exclamation of astonishment at the marvellous way in which the Old Testament prepares and prefigures the New? The truth is that, besides being Israel, Mary is also Christianity; she is the perfect Christian, the single person in all human history who knew how to respond best to God's Word and favor to her: "My soul proclaims the greatness of the Lord, for the Almighty has done great things for me" (Communion Antiphon). Do we want to know how to pray? Mary shows us how in her being as in her *Magnificat* (and Hannah didn't do so badly either). Next to the Eucharist and the Our Father, both prayers of Mary's Son Jesus, the *Magnificat* is the greatest.

We are getting ready for the celebration of the birth of the child Mary was carrying in her womb the day she gave us this prayer. Has it ever struck you how extraordinary was Mary's preparation for that birth? She doesn't withdraw from life into a cell all by herself. She works. She does Elizabeth's housework and cooking, and, though the Gospel doesn't tell us, we can be pretty sure she helped with the birth of Elizabeth's son and did some housecleaning before she returned home to await her own "happy event."

We need her example in just being ourselves, but being ourselves may require us to make our own the plea of today's Prayer Over the Gifts:

> By the mystery of this eucharist
> purify us and renew your life within us.

* * *

"My heart rejoices in the Lord, my Savior" *(Responsorial Psalm)*.

"My soul proclaims the greatness of the Lord, for the Almighty has done great things for me" *(Communion Antiphon)*.

"King of all nations,
source of your Church's unity and faith:
save all mankind, your own creation!" *(Gospel Verse)*.

READING I   **Mal 3:1-4, 23-24**
GOSPEL   **Luke 1:57-66**

Reading I: The prophet Malachi foretells the coming of a messenger who will prepare the way for God's own visit among his people.

Gospel: Luke describes the astonishing events that accompanied the birth and circumcision of John, the messenger envisioned by Malachi.

The birth of the Savior in Bethlehem was not at all unexpected. The Hebrew people had long been nourished on God's promises and prophecies which became more and more intense and specific as the "fullness of time" drew near. Today's Reading I gives some idea of the cause of this hope and expectation:

> Lo, I am sending my messenger
>   to prepare the way before me;
> And suddenly there will come to the temple
>   the Lord whom you seek,
> And the messenger of the covenant whom you desire.

The prophet then describes the work of the Lord whom they seek:

> He will sit refining and purifying,
>   and he will purify the sons of Levi . . . .
> that they may offer due sacrifice to the Lord.

Then the prophet identifies this messenger of the Lord as Elijah.

The Gospel relates the family celebration when Zechariah's and Elizabeth's relatives gather to celebrate the birth and circumcision of their only son. They all want to call the child after his father, but Elizabeth insists that the name will be John. And when Zechariah confirms his wife's decision, his mouth is opened and "he began to speak in praise of God." We'll hear Zechariah's song tomorrow.

What is astonishing is the reaction of the relatives at this marvellous happening: Fear descended not only on those present but on the whole neighborhood, and "throughout the hill country of Judea these happenings began to be recounted to the last detail" (Gospel). Obviously, they could sense that something great and extraordinary was about to take place. "All who heard stored these things in their hearts, saying 'What will this child be?'" And "Was not the hand of the Lord upon him?"

That divine hand was indeed upon John. He is to be the Elijah, the messenger who would prepare the way before the Lord. You people of the hill country and all who hope and look for the Savior of the world, "Lift up your heads and see; your redemption is near at hand" (Responsorial Psalm).

With all this marvellous imagery and prophecy fulfilled and stored in our minds and hearts, it is now time for us to leave history and reenter the present. Tomorrow night we are to celebrate the birth of the one responsible for all the excitement and mystification that filled the air at John's birth and circumcision. The words of the Responsorial Psalm are now addressed to us: "Lift up your heads and see; your redemption is near at hand." To be sure, redemption has already taken place. Christ did that when he came shortly after John and did the work for which John prepared the way.

We still live in a sin-laden world. Life is hard. Though redeemed, we are still capable of sin. There are still "unredeemed" areas of our lives that press us down. So today's psalm is as much our prayer as it was the prayer of the people who lived before Christ:

> Your ways, O Lord, make known to me;
> teach me your paths . . . .

Christmas is here. "A little child is born for us, and he shall be called the mighty God; every race on earth shall be blessed in him" (Entrance Antiphon). Now this child speaks to us: "I stand at the door and knock, says the Lord. If anyone hears my voice and opens the door, I will come in and sit down to supper with him and he with me" (Communion Antiphon).

Jesus makes the plea to you and to me. Can we possibly refuse him entrance into the house of our hearts? "Lord . . . prepare us to welcome your Son with ardent faith" (Prayer After Communion).

* * *

"Come, Emmanuel,
God's presence among us, our King, our Judge:
save us, Lord our God!" *(Gospel Verse).*

"Restore us to your peace
and prepare us to celebrate the coming of our Savior . . . ."
(Prayer Over the Gifts).

"I stand at the door and knock . . . . If anyone hears my voice and opens the door, I will come in and sit down to supper with him and he with me" *(Communion Antiphon).*

DECEMBER 24
MORNING MASS

READING I   2 Sam 7:1-5, 8-11, 16
GOSPEL   Luke 1:67-79

Reading I: We hear God's promise to David that he would build a "house" for him, a progeny that will endure till the end of time.

Gospel: The inspired Zechariah, liberated from his dumbness, burst out into song at the birth of his son John and what it will mean for all the world.

Our four weeks of preparation for the celebration of the Savior's birth are over. Please God that the excitement of family celebrations and "the holiday spirit" have not taken too much out of the deep spiritual content of these grace-filled days! It is one of the ironies of modern life that our greatest *religious* events have become so completely secularized that people celebrate without even knowing the reason why.

Christmas, of course, has to be celebrated, and the more joy, good will, and love we put into the celebration, the better. But the festiveness must not be allowed to obscure the true cause of it all, namely, God's *Christmas present,* the gift of his own Son to the world, to us—also the consequences of that gift for our life and happiness in this world and the world to come.

"The appointed time has come; God has sent his Son into the world" (Entrance Antiphon). It is that sending we celebrate tonight and tomorrow. So our prayer at this Mass is much to the point:

Come, Lord Jesus,
do not delay;
give new courage to your people who trust in your love.
By your coming, raise us to the joy of your kingdom . . . .

It's one of Advent's finest prayers—also one we really need answered this year. God knows our need for new courage in order to avoid being overcome by life's cares and burdens, and in our inmost hearts we also know that need. But perhaps an even greater need is for deeper trust in God's love, not only in this celebration but in the year ahead.

Then there is the petition:

By your coming,
raise us to the joy of your kingdom . . . .

In other words, purify, sanctify, or more exactly, *Christianize* the joy of our family celebrations and help us acknowledge in our hearts and lives that God and God alone is our true Lord, that he is the only Christmas present that does not grow old or wear out. "For ever I will sing the goodness of the Lord" (Responsorial Psalm). That's it! Forever, not just for a day or a month or a year, but forever.

It is the readings, of course, that give us the scriptural background for our celebration. The word "house" has several meanings, the most obvious being a building to dwell in. But it also means a family, a progeny, like "the house of David," or "the house of King Saul." Here God, through the prophet Nathan, has to remind David that *he* is the one who will build a house for David (not the other way around, as David mistakenly thought). It is to be a house that will last forever because its true head will be David's descendant Jesus, whose birth we celebrate tonight.

> Blessed be the Lord the God of Israel
> because he has visited and ransomed his people.
> He has raised a horn of saving strength for us
> in the house of David his servant . . . . (Gospel).

Besides reviewing God's past blessings to his people, Zechariah lays out a way of life for us who accept the newborn Savior into the *house* of our hearts:

> that, rid of fear and delivered from the enemy,
> We should serve him devoutly, and through all our days
> be holy in his sight.

"He has visited and redeemed his people" (Communion Antiphon). This is our cause, our reason, for rejoicing.

> May we who look forward to the feast of Christ's birth
> rejoice for ever in the wonder of his love . . . .
> (Prayer After Communion)

May we rejoice, not for just an hour or for a day or a week, but forever!

* * *

"For ever I will sing the goodness of the Lord" *(Responsorial Psalm).*

"he, the Dayspring, shall visit us in his mercy
To shine on those who sit in darkness and in the shadow of death,
to guide our feet into the way of peace" *(Gospel).*

"By our sharing in this eucharist
free us from sin" *(Prayer Over the Gifts).*

14   **CHRISTMAS**
                                    MASS AT MIDNIGHT

READING I Isa 9:1-3, 5-6   **READING II** Tit 2:11-14
GOSPEL   Luke 2:1-14

Reading I: Isaiah foretells what we already know:

> For a child is born to us, a son is given us . . . .
> They name him Wonder-Counselor, God-Hero,
>   Father-Forever, Prince of Peace.

Reading II: St. Paul provides us with the proper response in our life that
we ought to follow as a result of Christ's birth to us.

Gospel: We hear Luke's account of Jesus' birth in Bethlehem and the
announcement of the birth to poor shepherds watching their
flocks.

> Sing to the Lord a new song:
> sing to the Lord, all you lands.
> Sing to the Lord; bless his name. . . .
> Tell his glory among the nations . . . . (Responsorial Psalm).

This night in the City of David a Savior is born to us, the Messiah,
the Lord! This night.

> Good News and great joy to all the world;
> today is born our Savior, Christ the Lord (Gospel Verse).

Christmas is real. It is now. We celebrate a real event; it is not just
an echo, a remembering, of a long-past holy night.

For a few moments on Christmas, especially Christmas Eve,
most people feel just a little more "religious" than usual. God tries
in a thousand ways to speak to us, to penetrate our armor, telling us
about himself and his love for us. We often fail to hear his voice and
to grasp the fullness of his love for us, preoccupied as we often
become with so many things to do and say.

But in some mysterious way on Christmas Eve God succeeds
momentarily, and the story of the birth of a child in Bethlehem
reaches the very core of our being—drawing us out of our shells
into the realm of the divine. Tonight we catch a glimpse of the
mystery of divine splendor, of the infinite, the ineffable majesty
with whom we are destined to live forever—the one who is the fulfillment of all our Advent preparation and longing. Now we know
that all that longing and preparation were worthwhile.

We need to look at the readings in order to get some idea of
what the Lord wishes us to understand concerning this marvellous
birth. Reading I tells us that

98

the people who walked in darkness
have seen a great light;
Upon those who dwelt in the land of gloom
a light has shone.

Light is one of the great symbols of the divine, and how we and our world need it! This light shines into the mystery of the darkness of our lives. Our world is full of people who literally walk in the gloom of despair, "dwelling in the land of gloom." Think of all the lonely women, men, and children in our cities, towns, and the countrysides who seem to have no one to care for them. They must wonder why. Why all the loneliness, the pain, sorrow, grief they have to live with? Does Christmas have any meaning for them?

The child born of Mary tonight will not give any verbal answers to our questioning, our pain. He simply joins our human life, takes on our flesh and all the sorrow and pain connected with our lives. He will know by firsthand experience what human living means and involves. He will know much more vividly than we do ourselves. Christmas is essentially the story of God's-being-with-us in every moment of our lives. "The Word was made flesh," the Evangelist John will tell us in tomorrow's Mass. The Word took on our flesh, the flesh of all humankind.

I do not have the date of an article by Karl Rahner that appeared in the *National Catholic Reporter* many years ago. Rahner says:

> God has come. He is there in the world. And therefore everything is different from what we imagine it to be. Time is transformed from its eternal onward flow into an event that with silent, clear resoluteness leads to a definitely determined goal. . . . When we say, "It is Christmas," we mean that God has spoken into the world his last, his deepest, his most beautiful word in the incarnate Word, a word that can no longer be removed because it is God's definitive deed, because it is God himself in the world. And this means: I love you, you, the world and man . . . . I am there. I am with you. I am your life. I am your time. I am the gloom of your daily routine. Why will you not bear it?

The Gospel tells of the birth of Jesus that night in Bethlehem. "She gave birth to her first-born son and wrapped him in swaddling clothes and laid him in a manger, because there was no room for them in the place where travelers lodged." The eternal Son of God appears as a babe, the most helpless and dependent of all creatures. "God's folly is wiser than men, and his weakness more powerful than men," says St. Paul (1 Cor 1:25). God humbles himself to the point of total dependence. He comes to us intending to conquer our hearts through his own weakness. What he wants of us is not slavish obedience, but generous, freely-given love.

Then Reading II tells us that Christmas is just a beginning. Every Christmas is a beginning—that first one in Bethlehem and this one tonight. "The grace of God has appeared, offering salvation to all men. It trains us to reject godless ways and worldly desires and live temperately, justly, and devoutly in this age as we await our blessed hope, the appearing of the glory of the great God and of our Savior Jesus Christ." We await the blessed hope. Christmas is always a beginning.

In other words, the incarnation is not yet complete. The physical incarnation was completed and finished that night in Bethlehem. But not the "mystical" incarnation, that is, Christ's coming into each one of us, into our lives, our world. This still has to be realized in time—in the years and centuries ahead. As for us, all he wants is our Yes.

> Lord . . . .
> By our communion with God made man,
> may we become more like him
> who joins our lives to yours. . . . (Prayer Over the Gifts).

Becoming "more like him" takes time, but that's our destiny from now on.

On the first Christmas Jesus established contact between himself and us; now he seeks a response in love. Such is the mystery of communication we know as prayer, the mystery of identification between Christ and each of us until we are transformed into him totally. History, above all our personal history, is nothing else than Jesus' continuing act of love in quest of us all, his enduring declaration of love for us spoken into the depth of our hearts and our being.

> God our Father,
> we rejoice in the birth of our Savior.
> May we share his life completely
> by living as he has taught (Prayer After Communion).

* * *

"Let us all rejoice in the Lord, for our Savior is born to the world. True peace has descended from heaven" (Alternative Opening Antiphon).

"The people who walked in darkness
have seen a great light . . . ." (Reading I).

15   CHRISTMAS
MASS AT DAWN

READING I   Isa 62:11-12   **READING II**   Tit 3:4-7
GOSPEL   Luke 2:15-20

Reading I: The Lord proclaimed through the prophet Isaiah that the Savior comes, his reward with him.

Reading II: St. Paul tells Titus (and us) that God has saved us, not because of any righteous acts we have done but solely because of his mercy.

Gospel: In obedience to the angels' summons, the shepherds go to Bethlehem and thus become Jesus' first visitors.

This Mass has traditionally been called the ''Shepherds' Mass,'' the reason obviously being the Gospel account of the shepherds' being the first ones to be told of the birth of the Savior in a Bethlehem cave. Their response to the angels' announcement is so human and so perfect: ''Let us go over to Bethlehem and see this event which the Lord has made known to us.'' They went in haste, St. Luke tells us, and who wouldn't after the kind of news they had received and the kind of messengers who brought it! Angels—multitudes of them,

> praising God and saying:
> ''Glory to God in high heaven,
> peace on earth to those on whom his favor rests.''

So they went and they saw and Luke tells us they *understood* what had been told them concerning this child. Well, if they understood, they were far ahead of many of the wise and learned men and women who have since studied this event. Not only did the shepherds understand, they went out and told everyone about it. But then they went back to their work, but their lives could never again be the same because of what has happened. They glorified and praised God for all they had heard and seen ''in accord with what had been told them.''

Mary's reaction was quite different. We can be sure she smiled a welcome to these rough-looking men who had come to offer homage to her child. And then, when they left, she ''treasured all these things and reflected on them in her heart.'' Like Mary we, too, can and must treasure everything we have heard and witnessed not only in these Christmas Masses but in our entire Advent experience. Like Mary we have been engaged in a great adventure of faith and love. How better to react than by treasuring ''all these things in our hearts''? Not just remembering them from time to

101

time, but keeping them alive in our hearts and rejoicing in them. If we are moved to imitate the shepherds and tell everyone about God's loving visitation and what it has meant to us, so much the better.

> Lord,
> with faith and joy
> we celebrate the birthday of your Son.
> Increase our understanding and our love
> of the riches you have revealed in him . . . .
> (Prayer After Communion)

* * *

"A light will shine on us this day: the Lord is born for us" *(Responsorial Psalm)*.

"When the kindness and love of God our Savior appeared, he saved us . . . because of his mercy" *(Reading II)*.

"Mary treasured all these things and reflected on them in her heart" *(Gospel)*.

16　　　　　　　　　**CHRISTMAS**
　　　　　　　MASS DURING THE DAY

READING I　Isa 52:7-10　　　　　　**READING II**　Heb 1:1-6
GOSPEL　　John 1:1-18

Reading I:　"The Lord comforts his people, he redeems Jerusalem." Carried away by his vision, Isaiah cries: "All the ends of the earth will behold the salvation of our God."

Reading II:　The author of Hebrews gives the prophetic background of the marvellous event we are celebrating: after speaking through the prophets, God now speaks to us "through his Son . . . through whom he first created the universe."

Gospel:　The eternal Word, the everlasting Light is made flesh and dwells among us, and "we have seen his glory . . . ."

How beautiful upon the mountains are the feet of him who brings glad tidings, announcing peace, bearing good news, announcing salvation, and saying to Zion, "Your God is King!"

Every word in that prophecy of Isaiah demands reflection, especially "glad tidings," "announcing peace," "bearing good news," "announcing salvation, and saying to Zion, 'Your God is King.'" That last phrase takes us back to the beginning—to the first entrance of rebellion into human history when our first parents wanted to replace God with their own will: they wanted to be like unto God. Now, at long last the promised Savior is born, and his glad message is that our God is King and no one else. Humankind is once again reconciled with the Creator, and that's the best possible news. We are again reconciled with our God, we are redeemed, rescued:

> All the ends of the earth have seen the saving power of God.
> Sing to the Lord a new song, for he has done wondrous deeds . . . .
> (Responsorial Psalm).

"The Lord is King." That might well be the chief meaning of Christmas. The Lord is Lord, Ruler, supreme over all, but we are not slaves. So perhaps the chief meaning of Christmas is that we mean everything to him; we are his children and he loves us to such a degree that he gives us his only-begotten Son as our brother, our Savior, our Reconciler.

Christmas is all this—and more. At Midnight Mass our attention was concentrated on the humanity of Jesus, on the baby born of Mary and laid in a manger. And Reading I told us:

> For a child is born to us, a son is given us;
> upon his shoulders dominion rests.

His identity was established—Son of God, Son of Mary, fulfiller of all the divine promises and prophecies. In the Responsorial Psalm we sang: "Today is born our Savior, Christ the Lord."

In the Mass at Dawn we followed the shepherds, simplest of God's poor, to the Child's manger in Bethlehem, and Mary confided to us the secret of keeping Christmas in our lives, i.e., treasuring all these things and reflecting on them in our hearts. But there is another note in that second Christmas Mass that indicates a progressive understanding, not only of the identity of the Child but in the deep meaning of what it is all about—what the ultimate purpose of the birth really is. We pray in the Alternative Opening Prayer:

> Almighty God and Father of light . . . .
> Your eternal Word leaped down from heaven
> in the silent watches of the night,
> and now your Church is filled with wonder
> at the nearness of her God.

Open our hearts to receive his life
and increase our vision with the rising of dawn,
that our lives may be filled with his glory and his peace . . . .

So we have a bridge from Bethlehem's manger into a world that is still in the making and will not be finished until the Word is made flesh, that is, becomes one with humanity in every age and condition. This meaning is hinted at in the Opening Prayer of this Third Christmas Mass:

Lord God,
we praise you for creating man,
and still more for restoring him in Christ.
Your Son shared our weakness:
may we share his glory . . . .

We might modify or enlarge that idea and insist that he continues to share our weakness and will continue to share it until all humankind is filled with his glory at time's end. In other words, as Fr. Michael Quoist points out:

The mystery of the Incarnation is not yet complete. No doubt, the advent of God in a man's body and in human life—i.e., the physical or historical Incarnation—is complete. But the mystical incarnation, Jesus' coming into each man, into man's life and the life of the world . . . must still be realized in time by means of man's free response (*Christ Among Us*, Garden City, N.Y.: Doubleday and Co., 1971, 80).

We can only conclude that the Word being made flesh and *making his dwelling among us* is an inexhaustible mystery. Today's Gospel tells us:

He was in the world . . . .
To his own he came,
yet his own did not accept him.

What does this mean? Maybe that they simply did not understand what was the full meaning of "The Word became flesh," and most people still don't. They have seen it as being limited to Jesus' taking flesh in Mary's womb. Now we know it is much more: it is Christ joining himself to our lives, our sorrows and joys, our agonies and dyings. Christmas, we repeat, is only a beginning. That was the first Christmas, and it is the one we are now celebrating. This Christmas is a return to our roots, our source as Christians, but more than anything else it is an invitation to all of us to say YES and make our lives, and every moment, every aspect, of those lives more and more open to him.

We pray:

Make us faithful to your Word,
that we may bring your life to the waiting world.
(Alternative Opening Prayer)

May the Word become more and more flesh of our flesh and bone of our bone.

* * *

"All the ends of the earth will behold the salvation of our God" *(Reading I)*.

"In this, the final age, he [God] has spoken to us through his Son . . . ." *(Reading II)*.

"The Word became flesh and made his dwelling among us . . . ." *(Gospel)*.

696   **DECEMBER 26**
ST. STEPHEN

READING I   Acts 6:8-10; 7:54-59
GOSPEL   Matt 10:17-22

Reading I: The author of Acts relates how Stephen, "filled with grace and power, who worked great wonders and signs among the people," antagonizes some hearers and is put to death.

Gospel: Jesus predicts how his followers will be persecuted and tells them not to worry. "Whoever holds out till the end will escape death."

It is doubtful that Stephen ever heard Jesus' prophetic warning to his apostles about the persecution they will have to undergo for his sake. But everything Jesus predicted is fulfilled to the letter by this fearless holy young man, including Jesus' words: "When the hour comes, you will be given what you are to say. You yourselves will not be the speakers; the Spirit of your Father will be speaking in you."

Reading I does not tell all that Stephen says, so it would be worth reading all of Acts 7, for it reviews all the details of God's marvellous care of his people throughout their history, leading up to Christ. Stephen's "sermon" is a first-class example of how the apostles preached in those days. The "young man named Saul," at whose feet the murderers piled their cloaks, was very likely the Saul who was later converted, possibly by the courage, convictions, and the blood of Stephen, and came to be known as Paul. Paul would later preach in precisely the same way—by reviewing Sacred History, but he was much more successful in converting his hearers than Stephen.

So Stephen dies for Christ—reputedly the first martyr to shed his blood for Jesus. Somehow it seems appropriate to celebrate the birth of Stephen into heavenly life the very next day after we celebrate the birth of the Savior into the life of our world.

We do not know how or when Stephen was converted, but he was obviously so possessed by Jesus that he was "filled with grace and power . . ." and "worked great wonders and signs among the people" (Reading I). He was the perfect disciple to the very end. Even as he lay dying under the barrage of stones, he cried out: "Lord Jesus, receive my spirit." And then, "Lord, do not hold this sin against them" (Acts 7:60). Perfect disciple indeed! Not only did Jesus give his grace and courage to Stephen; he also made known to him how to die—and to live.

There is much for us to admire and imitate in Stephen's life and death. The least obvious but perhaps the essential thing is our relationship with Jesus, the intimacy of it, amounting to allowing him to possess us and all that we are and have. The rest will follow almost automatically, i.e., our making Stephen's dying prayer a prayer for living first, and then dying when Jesus is ready for us: "Lord Jesus, receive my spirit . . . ." (Reading I). "Into your hands, O Lord, I entrust my spirit" (Responsorial Psalm).

But perhaps even more important for our life now is the Christlike value Stephen demonstrated as he breathed his last: "Lord, do not hold this sin against them." It would be better for our peace of mind, to say nothing of the condition of our souls, if we would not wait with that sentiment and prayer till we are ready to meet Christ face to face. We can do it now. Stephen would like that!

* * *

"Lord, do not hold this sin against them" *(Acts 7:60)*.

"Into your hands, O Lord, I entrust my spirit" *(Responsorial Psalm)*.

DECEMBER 27
ST. JOHN, Apostle and Evangelist

READING I   **1 John 1:1-4**
GOSPEL   **John 20:2-8**

Reading I: Speaking as a member of the apostolic college, John claims that the foundation of their preaching is what they have seen and heard "of the word of life."

Gospel: John gives the account of his and Peter's arrival at Christ's empty tomb on that first Easter morning.

The majority of the apostles Jesus chose to be the foundation of his Church were ordinary men. But John was extraordinary in many ways—maybe not in the beginning but in his potential. He is one of the great examples in history of Christ's ability to bring forth the best in a person's basic, often undiscovered, talents.

John, like his brother James, was a fisherman, and in his early days as an associate of Jesus, he was an impetuous, ambitious politician-in-the-making. He and his brother even schemed to get their mother to ask Jesus to give them the highest positions in the kingdom they thought and hoped he would establish. When Jesus asked them if they could "drink the cup he would drink," they said, "We can," most probably not realizing what kind of commitment they were making.

There were many years between the John of those days and the mature and wonderfully learned John who wrote the Fourth Gospel some sixty years after he and Peter had raced to the empty tomb that first Easter morning (Gospel). The Gospel even indicates a development between John's plotting for the first place in the kingdom and the first Easter. John arrives at the tomb first because he was younger and a better runner (maybe even because he loved Jesus more) than Peter, but Peter had been Christ's choice to head the apostles and John deferred to him, allowing him to enter the tomb first.

Matthew, Mark, and Luke (the synoptic evangelists), during the course of the last third of the first century, recorded the early Christian communities' memories of what Jesus said and did. We can be grateful to them for the legacy they left us in their Gospels. John waited until he had meditated an entire lifetime on his personal memories of what Jesus had said and done—*on what Jesus had been to him personally;* and then, at the end of the century, in his Epistles and Gospel, he opens his heart and gives us a glimpse of that blessed remembrance:

What we have seen and heard
we proclaim in turn to you
so that you may share life with us. . . .
Indeed, our purpose in writing you this
is that our joy may be complete (Reading I).

Today's Mass gives us some idea of how John came to such an incredible development:

God our Father,
you have revealed the mysteries of your Word
through John the apostle (Opening Prayer).

Then the prayer reveals to us the way, the only one, by which we can share in John's glorious achievement:

By prayer and reflection
may we come to understand the wisdom he taught.

Is this an impossible dream? The lives of many Christian women and men who have followed this prescription prove that it is not.

But most of us are not contemplatives like John and all those other holy people who had all day to pray. What does John have for us? We have his Gospel and his letters. Perhaps if we gave ten or fifteen minutes a day to slow, reflective reading and praying of those writings (along with other New and Old Testament writings), we could arrive at a higher degree of contemplation than we have hoped for. May we not forget: we have the same Jesus John had—present to us as really and as truly through faith as he was to John. We also have the Eucharist—the same Eucharist that nourished John throughout his long life (after the Last Supper).

Lord,
bless these gifts we present to you.
With St. John may we share
in the hidden wisdom of your eternal Word
which you reveal at this eucharistic table (Prayer Over the Gifts).

John spent a lifetime meditating on Christ—on what he said and did, above all, on his person. John is still meditating because Jesus is the Word, inexhaustible in being and in meaning, for he is God. John has a head start on us, to be sure, but that start should not discourage us. What's two thousand years of head start when eternity lies ahead—for John as well as for us? The essential fact is this: "The Word of God became man, and lived among us. Of his riches we have all received" (Communion Antiphon).

Through this eucharist may your Son always live in us,
for he is Lord for ever and ever (Prayer After Communion).

* * *

"Blessed apostle, to you were revealed the heavenly secrets! Your lifegiving words have spread over all the earth!" *(Alternative Opening Antiphon)*.

"The Word of God became man, and lived among us. Of his riches we have all received" *(Communion Antiphon)*.

698   DECEMBER 28
HOLY INNOCENTS

READING I   1 John 1:5-2:2
GOSPEL   Matt 2:13-18

Reading I: John tells us that we are all sinners and need Christ. His main concern is to keep us from further sin.

Gospel: Matthew relates the flight of the Holy Family to Egypt and the massacre of the Holy Innocents—all male children under age two.

These innocent children were slain for Christ. They follow the spotless Lamb, and proclaim for ever: Glory to you, Lord.
(Entrance Antiphon)

A martyr is a person who, knowing the possible consequences, freely and deliberately bears witness to his/her faith in Christ and suffers death as a result of that witness. So it may be stretching the meaning of the word a bit to call a band of cruelly massacred helpless children, under age two, "martyrs," since they had no choice in the matter.

The essential fact, however, is that they died because of Christ: he was the occasion of their deaths; they gave their lives because of him, and I dare say that when they reached heaven and began to experience its wonders, they gladly gave a post-dated, free, and joyous consent. One of the early Fathers of the Church playfully pictured the Holy Innocents in heaven, playing at hoops with their martyrs' crowns. In any case, their deaths following so closely after the historical birth of Jesus, it is fitting that we celebrate the feast of their birth into heaven shortly after our celebration of the birth of Jesus into our world this and every year.

It may not be easy for us moderns to extend the spirit of joyous celebration proper to the feast of Christmas to a feast like this. That's probably all right. One thing the account of the massacre does provide for us a glimpse into the reality of the evil situation which Jesus entered when he became man. The killing of the children was a heinous crime—a dramatic symbol of the evil that confronted the Savior at the beginning of his life on earth and which he would combat all through his public life.

At the end of his public life, evil had apparently gained the victory, but we know that he rose from the dead, and "death was swallowed up by victory." Nevertheless, evil still exists and today it seems as powerful and deadly as ever. There can be no doubt that millions more innocent children are murdered now than by Herod's soldiers; worse than that, all humankind and the world we inhabit often seem close to total destruction. Was Christ a failure?

We don't have to point fingers at others. We need to look into our own hearts. St. John warns us in Reading I:

If we say, "We have never sinned,"
we make him [Christ] a liar
and his word finds no place in us.
My little ones,
I am writing this to keep you from sin.

No, despite the condition of human hearts everywhere, we cannot say that Christ has failed. He preached good news of God's love, a Gospel that points the way to the ultimate victory—his and ours together. The incarnation and redemption (as was pointed out in one of the Christmas Masses) are as yet incomplete, unfinished. Jesus left the implementation of redemption in the hands of humanity, of free persons. We do not know how many generations of that humanity remain. That's not our concern. What is our concern is that, because of us and the Christian witness we bear, the world will be better than when we came into it. We can rely on John's word:

We have, in the presence of the Father,
Jesus Christ, an intercessor who is just.

And he has the Holy Innocents and countless saints with him.

He is an offering for our sins,
and not for our sins only,
but for those of the whole world (Reading I).

* * *

"May our lives bear witness
to the faith we profess with our lips" (Opening Prayer).

"We praise you, God; we acknowledge you as Lord; the radiant army of martyrs acclaims you" *(Gospel Verse)*.

"These have been ransomed for God and the Lamb as the first-fruits of mankind; they follow the Lamb wherever he goes" *(Communion Antiphon)*.

203 DECEMBER 29
FIFTH DAY IN THE OCTAVE OF CHRISTMAS

READING I   1 John 2:3-11
GOSPEL   Luke 2:22-35

Reading I: John tells us that we cannot know Jesus unless we are willing to keep his commandments: to love God and to love our neighbor.

Gospel: Luke tells about the presentation of Jesus in the Temple forty days after his birth, and Simeon predicts that a sword will pierce Mary's heart.

Today's Mass recalls the recent past and also anticipates the not-too-distant future. Just a few days ago we celebrated the birth of Jesus, and the joyous afterglow of the feast will not fade away. Today's Entrance Antiphon brings home to us the reason for it all— God's Son would never have been made flesh at all were it not for the everlasting love of the Father *for us:* "God loved the world so much, he gave his only Son, that all who believe in him might not perish, but might have eternal life."

Both the Entrance Antiphon and Reading I remind us that this great gift has to have an effect in us and on us; otherwise it was all in vain and might as well never have happened. Our first obligation is to accept the gift and the love that prompted it. Most people are great at giving gifts but often hesitant about receiving them. Perhaps unconsciously we recognize that receiving gifts and so allowing oneself to be loved implies admitting a certain dependency on the giver. Being dependent on the Father is precisely what he wants us to be; it is precisely what we need to be—for our own good. Being dependent is not all, but it is at least part of the meaning of the word "believe" in the second part of the Entrance

Antiphon: "God . . . gave his only Son, that all who believe in him . . . might have eternal life."

Our celebration of Christ's birthday implies further obligations for us. In Reading I John speaks of our "knowledge of Jesus." Obviously, knowing Jesus implies more than knowing *about* him. It implies knowing him as a lover knows the beloved: knowing with mind and heart. It is knowledge penetrated with love. John tells us there is only one test for that kind of knowledge: keeping his commandments. Then the gentle John becomes explicit, even harsh:

> The person who claims, "I have known him,"
> without keeping his commandments,
> is a liar . . . .

Christ's commandments are now new. John reminds us that we've heard them more than once:

> The person who continues in the light
> is the one who loves his brother . . . .

At the beginning of this meditation, we said that this Mass anticipates the future. In the Gospel we are present at the presentation of Jesus in the Temple forty days after his birth. If this seems a little premature just now, let it be: it fits perfectly into the theme we have been considering—that of receiving love and allowing oneself to be loved.

If anyone knew how to receive gifts it was Mary. And old Simeon, too. Mary was the first one to receive God's gift and his love, and she responded with loving trust, total dependency, faith: "Be it done to me according to your word." Because Mary was so totally open to receiving, we can make our own the exclamation of the Mass today: "Let heaven and earth exult in joy" (Responsorial Psalm).

Simeon's reaction to being so loved is so beautiful that it has become the finest and most familiar evening prayer of Christians through the ages: He took the child in his arms and blessed God:

> Now, Master, you can dismiss your servant in peace . . . .
> For my eyes have witnessed your saving deed
>   displayed for all the peoples to see:
> A revealing light to the Gentiles,
>   the glory of your people Israel.

We are those Gentiles, to us the Light of the world has been revealed. "Through the tender compassion of our God, the dawn from on high shall break upon us" (Communion Antiphon). Let us rejoice and be glad!

* * *

"God loved the world so much, he gave his only Son . . . ." *(Entrance Antiphon)*.

"The person who continues in the light
is the one who loves his brother . . . ." *(Reading I)*.

Simeon took him in his arms and blessed God: "Now, Master, you can dismiss your servant in peace . . . ." *(Gospel)*.

204 **DECEMBER 30**
SIXTH DAY IN THE OCTAVE OF CHRISTMAS

When Christmas occurs on Sunday, the feast of the Holy Family (p. 117) is celebrated today.

READING I   1 John 2:12-17
GOSPEL   Luke 2:36-40

Reading I: John continues to preach to us about our obligations as Christians, in particular the obligation to be on our guard against worldliness.

Gospel: Anna, a prophetess, prayed as hard as Simeon for the Savior. When she finally sees him, she gives thanks to God and goes out and tells everybody about it.

When peaceful silence lay over all, and night had run half of her swift course, your all-powerful word, O Lord, leaped down from heaven, from the royal throne (Entrance Antiphon).

That is the immediate past, and the words are familiar to us from the Christmas Masses: "The Word became flesh and made his dwelling among us, and we have seen his glory . . . ."

Not satisfied with that recent memory, the Church takes us back today to Advent itself, to the conversion process we hopefully endured with the coaching of John the Baptist. John told us to prepare the way for the Savior's coming into our hearts by removing the roadblocks to malice, the curves and potholes of selfishness and sin. The Savior has come, so now we hope and pray that our celebration of his birth may complete what our efforts at penance and repentance began.

Retaining our spiritual gains along with making new progress in intimacy with Jesus, above all, warning against relapsing into our pre-Advent spiritual lukewarmness, is also John's concern in Reading I. First, there are a couple observations about John's style of writing. He seems to be speaking only to males, specifically to fathers and young men, also children. John *may* think all females are saints and do not need to be warned against worldliness, but it is more likely that he was simply a victim of the old-fashioned, but now distasteful, way of including all humans in the one noun "man."

The second observation is John's apparent hatred of "the world." What he is probably thinking of and condemning is worldliness or secularism. This is the kind of life led by people who exclude God and neighbor entirely from their thinking, people whose only goals in life are financial and social success: getting ahead at any cost—a "life of empty show" (Reading I).

John pleads with us all not to allow ourselves to slip back into such fatal and destructive philosophies of life. They make no sense because

> the world with its seductions is passing away
> but the one who does God's will
> endures forever.

A real grace resulting from our Advent-Christmas celebration would be for us to take these warnings to heart, so as not to have to learn the hard way. May we rather "come to live more fully the love we profess" (Prayer Over the Gifts).

The Gospel is a continuation of yesterday's. Mary and Joseph had heard Simeon's response to the Savior's arrival, and now we hear Anna's. "She gave thanks to God and talked about the child to all who looked forward to the deliverance of Jerusalem" (Gospel). She deserves more credit (and imitation) than is ordinarily given her.

So Christmas is still with us and we are still with Christmas. "Let heaven and earth exult in joy" (Responsorial Psalm). "From his riches we have all received, grace for grace" (Communion Antiphon). Christmas without an Octave just wouldn't be the same—or enough.

* * *

"A holy day has dawned upon us . . . .
Today a great light has come upon the earth" *(Gospel Verse)*.

"The child grew in size and strength, filled with wisdom, and the grace of God was upon him" *(Gospel)*.

205 **DECEMBER 31**
SEVENTH DAY IN THE OCTAVE OF CHRISTMAS

READING I 1 John 2:18-21
GOSPEL   John 1:1-18

Reading I: John warns strongly against the "antichrists" who refuse to understand Christ and who lead the people away from the true faith.

Gospel: Again we hear the familiar Prologue of John's Gospel telling us that Jesus is the Word of God made flesh, "and we have seen his glory."

> In the wonder of the incarnation
> your eternal Word has brought to the eyes of faith
> a new and radiant vision of your glory.
> In him we see our God made visible
> and so are caught up in love of the God we cannot see.
> (Preface of Christmas I)

Again we meditate on the wonderful exchange or contrast between Christ existing before all ages, made flesh on the first Christmas, and the effect his birth had on the world only a few generations later.

Much of this text is known to us already from the three Christmas Masses, but we can never hear too often the stirring words of the Entrance Antiphon: "A child is born for us, a son given to us; dominion is laid on his shoulders, and he shall be called Wonderful-Counselor." We can add from Isaiah's whole text: "The prince of peace." That was the vision of Isaiah some seven hundred years before the birth of Jesus.

John's vision gives the authentic identity of the child in deep theological language: In the beginning was the Word who was God, second Person of the Trinity; through him all things came into being. That is, in him, infinite, limitless Wisdom, was found the blueprint of all creation.

> The Word became flesh
> and made his dwelling among us,
> and we have seen his glory:
> The glory of an only Son coming from the Father,
> filled with enduring love (Gospel).

That's the true theological statement of who and what Jesus was and is—the statement of his identity. Reading I gives some idea of how necessary was that kind of theological precision. John writes about "antichrists" who appeared towards the end of the

115

first century, false teachers who actually denied that "Jesus is the Christ" (1 John 2:22). Knowing Jesus as he did and realizing the potential damage to the Savior's teaching that could result from such false interpretations of his message, John simply had to denounce the false teachers in the strongest possible terms. They are liars, antichrists, who had never really been Christians.

We do not know if it was that kind of false teaching that influenced John to write his Gospel and provide us with the familiar statement of Jesus' true identity, to say nothing of the deep meaning of his Gospel. John's letters and his Gospel were apparently written about the same time. There can be no question about the source of all John's writing—his personal knowledge of Jesus gathered during his association with him for three years, together with the deeper insights into the mystery of Christ resulting from many decades of meditation on his memories. John knew Jesus as no other human could have known him, save, of course, Mary his mother. To see and hear his beloved Master falsified and vilified made him very angry indeed.

It's time for us to come out of history into the present—into our ongoing celebration of Jesus' birth this year. Our Opening Prayer is a lesson in theology:

> Ever-living God,
> in the birth of your Son
> our religion had its origin and its perfect fulfillment.

It also points to the effect this birth ought to have in our lives:

> Help us to share in the life of Christ
> for he is the salvation of mankind . . . .

There is only one way to "share in the life of Christ," and that is to allow him to love others through us. We ought to give it a try.

* * *

"Sing to the Lord; bless his name;
  announce his salvation day after day" *(Responsorial Psalm)*.

"The Word became flesh
and made his dwelling among us . . . .
And who did accept him
he empowered to become children of God" *(Gospel)*.

"God's love for us was revealed when he sent his only Son into the world, so that we could have life through him" *(Communion Antiphon)*.

HOLY FAMILY
SUNDAY IN THE OCTAVE OF CHRISTMAS

When Christmas occurs on Sunday, the feast of Holy Family is celebrated on December 30.

READING I	Sir 3:2-6, 12-14	**READING II** Col 3:12-21
GOSPEL	Matt 2:13-15, 19-23	

Reading I: Sirach sets forth the Old Testament ideal of family life, an ideal that emphasizes mutual obligations and the rewards in store for those who fulfill their obligations.

Reading II: Paul's ideal for family living is based on mutual love and respect for and between each member of the family.

Gospel for Cycle A: Matthew relates his account of the sojourn of the Holy Family in Egypt and their return to Israel where they settle in Nazareth.

NOTE: *Comments on the Gospels for Cycles B and C follow this meditation.*

Most feasts celebrate *events* like the birth of Christ, his death and resurrection. Some feasts, on the other hand, celebrate ideals. The Feast of the Holy Family is one of these—and surely one of the most useful and necessary in any age, our own, above all. The feast involves much more than a nostalgic effort of the imagination to reconstruct the family life of Jesus, Mary, and Joseph and to propose their life together as a model for family life today—except for certain aspects of their life that never become out of date, as we shall see.

We simply do not know details of the daily living of the holy family, but we can certainly assume that it was just like the daily living of any other Jewish family in that particular era. The Gospel of Cycle A tells us nothing of their early life except that they began it as fugitives and, after a certain length of time, returned to their homeland and settled in Nazareth.

Both of the Opening Prayers emphasize ideals as well as petitions:

Father,
help us to live as the holy family,
united in respect and love.

Respect—actually *reverence* would be a more exact term—for the dignity of the person, from a tiny baby to an aged grandparent, is based on the truth that each is made in God's own image and so reflects his holiness and glory. Love follows respect. It implies living for, serving, sacrificing for others, in imitation of Jesus, God's Son, washing the feet of his disciples. With those two virtues as a conscious ideal for every member of any family, it is hard to imagine the family failing to grow together in joy and peace, on its way "to the joy and peace of your [the Father's] eternal home" (Opening Prayer).

The Alternative Opening Prayer is just as deserving of grateful reflection as the first:

> Teach us the sanctity of human love,
> show us the value of family life,
> and help us to live in peace with all men
> that we may share in your life for ever.

This prayer tells us that all human love, including the sexual love that exists between wife and husband, is *holy* and it can help parents to become more and more holy. It seems apparent that many couples have to learn this truth, and there is no better teacher than the one whose idea it was in the first place.

So there is something in this feast—in the writings and prayers —for everyone, including those whose parents have become aged and helpless:

> My son, take care of your father [mother, too] when he is old . . . .
> Even if his mind fail, be considerate with him . . . . (Reading I).

We must not allow the single sexist sentence in Reading II ("You who are wives, be submissive to your husbands") to spoil the beautiful ideal for family living that is presented in the rest of the reading. Paul proposes a way of life based on respect for the human person of whatever age (for all are "God's chosen ones, holy and beloved"), with the whole way of life shot through with love which "binds the rest together and makes them perfect." This ideal of family living is the only possible human response to God's having chosen us "as members of the one body [i.e., the body of Christ]" who "have been called to that peace."

There can be no family life of any kind without a sacrificial love on the part of each member. Family (and any community) life has to be made, created. And that is hard. Love is hard because it requires the decentralizing of self; it demands living for others instead of for oneself. And every member of the family bears responsibility for the success of the entire family effort.

Married life alone (without children) is difficult, and it cannot reach its full flowering without divine help. All the more is this the case with a larger family living together. St. Paul gives the secret of happiness for any family, a secret that is possible with a bit of cooperation on the part of all the members:

Let the word of Christ, rich as it is, dwell in you. . . . Sing gratefully to God from your hearts in psalms, hymns, and inspired songs. Whatever you do, whether in speech or in action, do it in the name of the Lord Jesus. Give thanks to God the Father through him.

It all sounds so beautiful, and so simple. Maybe that's why it is so seldom tried in families. Maybe a little communication between members (one idea St. Paul missed in his recipe for a happy family life) would help. Is it too late to start?

May this communion strengthen us
to face the troubles of life (Prayer After Communion).

* * *

"May the peace of Christ reign in your hearts;
and the fullness of his message live within you" (Gospel Verse).

"Father,
help us to live as a holy family,
united in respect and love" (Opening Prayer).

NOTE: The readings for Cycles B and C are the same as for Cycle A, except for the Gospels.

CYCLE B: Luke 2:22-40

Today's Gospel, about the presentation of Jesus in the Temple, has its own insights into the ideal Christian family life. Besides Mary, Joseph, and Jesus, it features two old people, Simeon and Anna, who had been waiting and praying for the coming of the Messiah all their lives. Now their waiting is rewarded: they hold him in their arms! One moral for family life is that old people, especially grandparents, need children, and children need grandparents—and old people. But even more important is the fact that Mary came to the Temple to offer, to present, her Child to the Lord from whom he came. And Simeon tells Mary that she herself shall be pierced with a sword. All family life is a mixture of joy and sadness—the greatest, the holiest family the world has known being no exception.

CYCLE C: Luke 2:41-52

Today's Gospel relates the story of Jesus (age twelve) and his parents in Jerusalem for the celebration of the greatest of Jewish feasts, the Passover. The details are familiar: Jesus stays behind,

119

Mary and Joseph discover his absence from their traveling group and return to seek him frantically for three days, finally finding him in the Temple, listening to the teachers and asking them questions.

"Son, why have you done this to us? You see that your father and I have been searching for you in sorrow." Jesus answers his mother: "Why did you search for me? Did you not know I had to be in my Father's house?" But they did not grasp what he said to them. We can be sure that now Mary has something else to reflect on in her heart.

This interchange of questions between Jesus and his parents often takes place in modern families. "They did not grasp what he said to them." This could well be the condition of many parents today when their teenagers want to try their wings. But lest these teenagers take Jesus as a model for their premature freedom ventures, let them remember that Jesus "went down with them, and came to Nazareth and was obedient to them."

"Jesus, for his part, progressed steadily in wisdom and age and grace before God and men." We can be sure that he had plenty of practical help and guidance from his foster father Joseph. Parents are still the greatest and best teachers, and if they teach only by example, so much the better.

18   JANUARY 1   OCTAVE OF CHRISTMAS
SOLEMNITY OF MARY, MOTHER OF GOD

READING I   Num 6:22-27   READING II   Gal 4:4-7
GOSPEL   Luke 2:16-21

Reading I: The Lord himself tells Moses and Aaron how he wants his people to be blessed—a blessing that cannot be improved upon.

Reading II: St. Paul informs us of our great dignity as members of Christ: we are adopted children of God, not slaves.

Gospel: Again we hear the familiar story of the shepherds' visit to Jesus in the manger, of Mary's personal reaction to what has taken place, and of the circumcision of Jesus eight days after his birth.

The Church seems to have had a hard time establishing an identity for this feast. I have an old missal that states that today's liturgy celebrates three feasts—the Octave day of Christmas, a feast honoring Mary's motherhood, and finally the feast of Jesus' circumcision. The new liturgy decreed by Vatican II now calls this the Octave of Christmas, the Solemnity of Mary, Mother of God. We can settle for that.

Then, of course, it is also New Year's Day, and the Church still thinks her children ought to begin a new year by being present at holy Mass. Like Christmas itself, the religious part of the day has a lot of competition from the very unliturgical, secular celebrations the world thinks are necessary in order to say farewell to an old year and welcome to the new one. So pastors hope for the best on New Year's morning.

"Hail, holy Mother! The child to whom you gave birth is the King of heaven and earth for ever" (Alternate Entrance Antiphon). The first meaning of the word "hail" in the dictionary is "to shout in greeting, welcome: cheer." That's much stronger than the simple "hello" meaning we usually give the word. It isn't hard to greet Mary with the full, most expansive meaning of our "Hail!" today. She's been somewhat in the background since all our attention was centered on her Son's birth eight days ago.

So it is fitting that she now receive her full measure of enthusiastic, loving gratitude from us for her part in bringing Jesus to us. Not that she wants any recognition, or needs it. Like the praise we give to God, our praise and love for Mary does more good for us than for her—it "makes us grow in grace" (IV Weekday Preface).

Today's prayers, especially the Opening Prayers and the Prayer After Communion, tell us everything about the reasonableness of our emphasis on Mary at this time. Along with our praise and grateful love for Mary, we cannot help thinking of her in connection with our needs as God's people and of each of us who are members of that people. As a people, a Church, we are still on our pilgrimage way towards the final goal in "restoring all things in Christ," the final goal of her Son's incarnation. We run into a lot of obstacles from within ourselves and without. Each of us has personal problems that require a mother's comforting prayer and guidance.

The Alternative Opening Prayer is very practical. We pray:

May her prayer, the gift of a mother's love,
be your people's joy through all ages.
May her response, born of a humble heart,
draw your Spirit to rest on your people.

The Prayer After Communion tells us how she is our mother:

Father,
as we proclaim the Virgin Mary
to be the mother of Christ and the mother of the Church,
may our communion with her Son
bring us to salvation.

We may wonder if this is the first time the liturgy makes use of the Vatican II title for Mary, "Mother of the Church." It is a title that brings us up-to-date in the evolution of Christian devotion to Mary: Mother of Christ, Mother of the Church. That's us—sisters and brothers of her Son.

But we can't let the feast go by without a mention of the circumcision of Jesus, which we also celebrate today. Circumcision is an ancient tribal practice of initiation, which the Hebrews converted into a religious rite. Abraham received it as a sign of the covenant between God and his people. So Jesus' circumcision marks him forever as a member of the Hebrew people, this Jesus who was "born of a woman, born under the law, to deliver from the law those who were subjected to it, so that we might receive our status as adopted sons" (Reading II).

Jesus sheds his blood for the first time. I am reminded of the words of the French novelist Leon Bloy: "The blood shed on the cross and the blood shed each day on our altars is naturally and supernaturally Jewish blood. It is part of that immense stream that has its source in Abraham and its mouth in the five wounds." A few drops now, a flood on the Cross. Blood, the sign of life. By his blood we are saved, we have life, divine life in us. What more fitting name could Joseph and Mary give him? Jesus, i.e., Savior, for he will save his people from their sins. Salvation is on its way: the blood shed at the circumcision is the first visible sign.

May we like Mary treasure all these things and reflect on them in our hearts!

* * *

"Hail, holy Mother! The child to whom you gave birth is the King of heaven and earth for ever" (Alternative Entrance Antiphon).

"The Lord look upon you kindly and give you peace!" (Reading I).

"Jesus Christ is the same yesterday, today, and for ever" (Communion Antiphon).

EPIPHANY

READING I	Isa 60:1-6	READING II Eph 3:2-3, 5-6
GOSPEL	Matt 2:1-12	

Reading I: The prophet foresees the glorious return of exiles to Jerusalem, but the vision really envisions the coming together of Jesus and the Gentiles in the person of the three astrologers.

Reading II: Paul reveals the secret of his apostolate: he is sent by God to proclaim the Good News of salvation to the Gentiles, whom God had chosen to be co-heirs of the kingdom with the Jews.

Gospel: We are present at the arrival in Bethlehem of the three astrologers who come with gifts to adore their Lord.

The real celebration of the incarnation for the Eastern Churches—both Uniate and Orthodox—is the Epiphany. This feast actually had a higher ranking in the "old" liturgy of our Latin rite than Christmas. For us the Epiphany is sort of an anti-climax, perhaps because it lacks the emotional or sentimental aura that has developed through the centuries around the feast of Christmas. Epiphany is obviously more "theological," more mind-expanding. Thank God we can have them both!

The idea of light dominates the liturgy of the feast. Light—the universal symbol of showing the way, of illumination, of warmth and beauty, of all that is implied in the concept of rescue, of salvation. "We have seen his star at its rising, and have come to pay him homage." The three astrologers are guided to salvation by the light of the star. In today's Preface we address the Father:

> Today you revealed in Christ your eternal plan of salvation
> and showed him as the light of all peoples.
> Now that his glory has shone among us
> you have renewed humanity in his immortal image.

If there is one idea this feast demonstrates, it is that Christianity, the overflow of the mind and vision of Jesus, is anything but narrow or provincial. Let us not forget that the astrologers came from the pagan nations and that they were themselves pagans. That's terribly significant. It means that the Chosen People, the Jews, are not the only ones chosen. There is something else: these Gentiles, even without the direct divine communication with the Creator that had been granted to the Hebrews, had some awareness of their need for God. They hungered for God and their hunger drove them on this long journey. Today we celebrate the manifesta-

123

tion of *God's* universal hunger and love for all peoples, regardless of nation, race, area.

All persons of all races are called to share in the glorious love of God revealed in Christ Jesus our Lord. One of the special graces of Epiphany for us is that of taking to ourselves God's universalist vision, his as yet unfulfilled desire to be known and loved by all humankind. What is true of Christmas is especially true of the Epiphany. The historical incarnation is indeed complete. But the mystical incarnation and self-manifestation, the *incarnation of Christ in all of society,* is still to be realized. The Catholic Church is as yet far from being truly or fully Catholic, fully universal.

We notice that there is an exchange of gifts, and it is indeed a wondrous one. The three visitors receive a life-changing revelation of the mystery and love of the one true God and his being, and in return they bring him the riches of their own lands. This is significant. We might well conclude from this incident that Catholicism will never be truly universal, never fully Catholic, until it has been enriched by the particular cultural and even religious characteristics and riches of all the nations and continents, especially Africa and India. One thinks, for example, of the contemplative spirit that is so prevalent in the Far East.

We pray in the Responsorial Psalm:

> Lord, every nation on earth shall adore you. . . .
> May he rule from sea to sea
>   and from the River to the ends of the earth.

I suppose that ideas like the above do not necessarily warm the heart, and this feast is supposed to be heart-warming as well as mind-expanding. We say that the astrologers received a revelation of the Child's divinity and lordship. I suspect that this revelation was more than an intellectual uplift. It must have touched their hearts, their entire being. Never again would their lives be the same. They had come as God-seekers, and now they rejoice in being God-finders.

We shouldn't be too afraid to use our imagination and try to reconstruct the scene in the cave that night. We can hear one of the Magi say: "We brought you some gifts." They hand over to Joseph the gold, the frankincense, and the myrrh because Jesus is too young to receive the gifts himself. But he is not too young to accept the love, the self-giving, the desire for him that the gifts symbolize, the gifts that brought these travelers to his side. He is a child, he loves to receive gifts. He is God, he loves to receive love.

Something similar can happen to us as we prepare to celebrate this feast. We don't have gold, frankincense, and myrrh to offer him. What we do have is much more precious in his sight: it is our lives, our hearts, our love for him and for one another. There is no limit to the depth and vastness of the experience of God and of the divine that this feast can bring us, but only on condition that we come seeking, bearing with us the gifts of our yearning hearts.

> Father of light, unchanging God,
> today you reveal to men of faith
> the resplendent fact of the Word made flesh.
> Your light is strong,
> your love is near;
> draw us beyond the limits which this world imposes,
> to the life where your Spirit makes all life complete (Opening Prayer).

The Church gives us this most daring of prayers today. May we not be afraid to make it our own. God's response might well become the most exciting experience of the divine we have had for a long time.

* * *

"Rise up in splendor, Jerusalem! Your light has come, the glory of the Lord shines upon you" *(Reading I)*.

"In Christ Jesus the Gentiles are now co-heirs with the Jews, members of the same body and sharers of the promise through the preaching of the gospel" *(Reading II)*.

"Go and get detailed information about the child" *(Gospel)*.

SUNDAY AFTER JANUARY 6
BAPTISM OF THE LORD

In those countries where Epiphany is transferred to a Sunday that falls on January 7, 8, or 9, the Baptism of the Lord is transferred to the Monday immediately following.

READING I Isa 42:1-4, 6-7   **READING II** Acts 10:34-38
GOSPEL   Matt 3:13-17

Reading I: We hear one of Isaiah's "servant songs" which foretells the relationship between God and the Messiah and the kind of work he will do.

Reading II: In an address to Cornelius and his guests, Peter presents a short review of the public life of Jesus, beginning with his baptism by John.

Gospel: We hear Matthew's account of Jesus' baptism by John and of the manifestation of the three Persons of the Trinity.

NOTE: *The prayers, psalms, and the readings of this feast are the same for all three cycles. Only the Gospels are different (Matthew, Mark, Luke), but each describes the essential features of the baptism of Jesus by John in the Jordan.*

There is a wealth of meaning in this event. First, there is a theophany, a manifestation of the divine, in this case of the three persons of the Trinity—the voice of the Father, the Son being baptized, and the Holy Spirit hovering over the Son in the form of a dove. The entire event is a catechesis for us, a dramatic instruction telling us about Jesus, who he was and is and what his work and destiny will be. But it also tells us about the kind of lives we, the followers of Jesus, are expected to live.

Jesus poses as a sinner here. He comes to John the Baptizer to submit to the ritual that identifies him with sinful humanity. John objects and tries to turn him away. Jesus insists: "Give in for now. We must do this if we would fulfill all of God's demands."

What does Jesus mean? Simply that it is fitting and necessary for him to do the will of the Father in all things, even to the point of identifying himself with sinful, unredeemed humanity. Here at the beginning of his public life he proclaims to all the world the inner dynamism, the basic motivation, of his entire life. His Father's will is to mean everything to him, and he will obey that will lovingly and freely. We cannot insist too strongly on his identifying himself with sinful humanity—with its pain, sorrow, grief, burdens, worries, as well as its guilt. There is a mysterious reality here that can easily escape us so that we might think that he's acting *as if* he were

21

a sinner. But Paul tells us: "For our sakes God made him who did not know sin, to be sin, so that in him we might become the very holiness of God" (2 Cor 5:21).

All this gives us some idea of the love Christ had for us all. "Love does such things." This universal suffering and dying of all humankind which Jesus takes upon himself may well be the main suffering of Jesus in his Passion. This idea is from Fr. Michael Quoist, who writes:

> Jesus, because he has infinite love for all and is aware of every person, saw, knew and suffered all of man's sufferings. With the weight of these sufferings on his back, he made his way to the cross. His cross was the wooden cross of the gospels; but it was also, and above all, the gigantic cross which has been erected at the center of human history. . . . When Jesus said, "Father, into thy hands I commit my spirit," it was a spirit enriched with all of humanity, past, present, and future. It was all of human history, and all of creation, now reoriented by Love towards eternal Love. It was the redemption of the world (Christ Is Alive, Garden City, N.Y.: Doubleday and Co., Inc., 1971, 101).

So, it is all this that Jesus' baptism previews. Back of it all, inspiring it all, is the undying love of the Father for all of us, his children. God so loved the world that he gave his only Son. The Son accepts his vocation. The Father's voice is heard: "This is my beloved Son. My favor rests on him." The vision of Isaiah is fulfilled:

> Here is my servant whom I uphold,
>   my chosen one with whom I am pleased,
> Upon whom I have put my spirit . . . .
> A bruised reed he shall not break,
>   and a smoldering wick he shall not quench . . . . (Reading I).

I said earlier that Jesus' baptism tells us about the kind of lives we are expected to live. Hopefully by now we understand that we do not live our lives alone. His self-identification with us at his baptism tells us that he is an essential part of our lives, with all that is in them, as we are part of his.

Another thought is to be found in today's Alternative Opening Prayer:

> May all who share in the sonship of Christ
> follow in his path of service to man,
> and reflect the glory of his kingdom
> even to the ends of the earth.

Jesus was the servant of servants. The Church is a servant Church; she reflects the life of her founder. We are members of Christ the servant, of his servant Church. The conclusion for us is clearly evident.

Finally, our meditation on the baptism of Jesus would be incomplete without seeing the Holy Spirit as essential to the baptism. The Holy Spirit will guide Jesus throughout his public life, as the Gospels indicate, and at the end of that life Jesus will promise to send that same Spirit to his Church, to us, to help us understand all that he will have said and done. As Jesus accepts and welcomes the Spirit at his baptism, so do we as we celebrate that baptism today. May that Spirit enable us all to accept Christ's and the Father's love, for it is only in receiving love that we will be made capable of giving it back.

> Almighty, eternal God,
> when the Spirit descended upon Jesus,
> at his baptism in the Jordan,
> you revealed him as your own beloved Son.
> Keep us, your children born of water and the Spirit,
> faithful to our calling (Opening Prayer).

By doing our best to be faithful to *our* calling, we can be sure of hearing the voice of the Father saying to us: "You are my beloved child. My favor rests on you."

* * *

"Here is my servant whom I uphold, my chosen one with whom I am pleased" *(Reading I)*.

"The heavens were opened and the Father's voice was heard: this is my beloved Son, hear him" *(Gospel Verse)*.

"This is he of whom John said: I have seen and have given witness that this is the Son of God" *(Communion Antiphon)*.